E. W. Bentley

The Classic of Orange

An historical discourse read before the Classis at its meeting in the

Reformed (Dutch) Church, Port Jervis, April 20, 1875

E. W. Bentley

The Classic of Orange
An historical discourse read before the Classis at its meeting in the Reformed (Dutch) Church, Port Jervis, April 20, 1875

ISBN/EAN: 9783337308285

Printed in Europe, USA, Canada, Australia, Japan

Cover: Foto ©ninafisch / pixelio.de

More available books at **www.hansebooks.com**

THE CLASSIS OF ORANGE

AN

Historical Discourse

Read before the Classis at its Meeting in the

REFORMED (DUTCH) CHURCH,

PORT JERVIS,

APRIL 20, 1875,

BY REV. E. W. BENTLEY,

PASTOR OF THE

REFORMED (DUTCH) CHURCH,

ELLENVILLE.

ELLENVILLE, N. Y.:

JAMES O. FISHER, STEAM BOOK AND JOB PRINTER.

1875.

The Classis of Orange.

This, now the largest of the Classes of the Reformed (Dutch) church, is an offshoot from the old Classis of Ulster. That Classis itself grew out of a division of the still older Classis of Kingston ordered by General Synod at its session in Albany in June, 1800, in the following terms :

"*Resolved :* That the Classis of Kingston be divided into two separate Classes to be known and distinguished by the names of the Classis of Poughkeepsie and the Classis of Ulster, and that the churches included within the bounds of the proposed Classis of Ulster do meet by their delegates on the 2nd day of September, 1800, and that the Rev. Stephen Goetschius preach on the occasion, and organize the Classis." The Ministers and Elders accordingly assembled at the time appointed at Marbletown, and Mr. G. preached from Isa., 26 : 2. "Open ye the gates, that the righteous nation which keepeth the truth may enter in."

The resolution of Synod did not specify the churches that were to constitute the new organization, but the roll of Classis on this occasion is as follows :

SHAWANGUNK,	Rev. Moses Freleigh,
MONTGOMERY,	Allard Anthony, Elder.
NEW PALTZ,	Rev. John H. Meier,
NEW HURLEY,	Christian Deyo, Elder.
CATSKILL,	Rev. Peter Labaugh,
OAK HILL,	John Souser, Elder.
ROCHESTER,	Rev. Gerritt Mandeville,
WAWARSING,	Elder's name illegible.
MARBLETOWN,	Rev. Stephen Goetschius, Abr'm Cantine, Elder.
SAUGERTIES,	(Caatsban) Absent,
ASHOKAN,	do.

4

It will be seen at a glance that the Classis covered a region of magnificent distances. Seventy-five years ago population was sparse, and centers were far apart. Hence the churches were scattered, and in most cases small and weak. Even those which united in the support of a pastor were in many instances so far asunder that they could enjoy services only upon alternate Sabbaths. The eleven churches which constituted the original Classis of Ulster occupied a territory stretching from Montgomery on the South to Catskill on the North, and from the Shandaken Mountains on the West to the Hudson River on the East. But the increase of population, and the law of growth enforced by the great head of the church, in a third of a century had just doubled the number of the churches in this region. When the Classis of Orange was formed in 1833, the mother Classis contained twenty-two churches, viz: Ashokan, Berea, Bloomingburgh, Bloomingdale, Dashville, Esopus, Fallsburgh, Flatbush, Hurley, Kingston, Mamakating, Marbletown, Montgomery, New Hurley, New Prospect, Clove, Rochester, Saugerties, Shawangunk, Wawarsing and Woodstock. Meantime, also of the original number, Catskill had been set off to the Classis of Rensselaer, and Oak Hill to the Classis of Schoharie. It will be seen at a glance that a body whose extremities were so far apart would be unwieldly. To attend a meeting of Classis in Montgomery would be no light task for the dominies of Shokan and Woodstock, when as yet Robert Fulton was but a "dreamer of dreams," and railroads had not been dreamed of at all. But aside from the matter of convenience, a more thorough oversight of the field required the separation. It was time for the hive to swarm again.

Accordingly, at the semi-annual meeting of the Classis in April, 1833, it was agreed that the Particular Synod should be asked to divide the body. This request was favorably received, as the following extract from the minutes of Particular Synod will show:

"On the Minutes of the Classis of Ulster is contained a re-

5

quest to divide said Classis, and to organize a new Classis to be called the Classis of Orange.   Whereupon,

Resolved, That the above application be granted according to request of the Classis, and that the new Classis be organized at the time and in the manner requested by the Classis of Ulster, and that the Clerk of Synod be requested to forward to the stated Clerk of the Classis of Ulster a copy of the foregoing resolutions.

A true extract from the minutes of the Particular Synod of Albany.

B. B. WESTFALL, } Clerks."
ABR. FORT,

In the application to Synod the Churches to be embraced in the new Classis were specified and provision made for the organization. Accordingly, on the Twenty-Second of May, 1833, the following persons met at the parsonage of the Montgomery Church, viz: Rev. R. P. Lee of the Church of Montgomery ; Rev J. H. Bevier of the Church of Shawangunk ; Rev. S. VanVechten of the Church of Bloomingburgh ; Rev. J. B. TenEyck of the Church of Berea ; Rev. A. J. Swits of the Church of Wawarsing, and the Elders Peter B. Cromwell of Berea ; John A. Schoonmaker of Shawangunk, and Samuel Hunter of Montgomery. By the order of Synod Rev. J. H. Bevier presided and preached ; Rev. A. J. Swits was chosen Clerk, Rev. J. B. TenEyck, Stated Clerk, and Rev. S. VanVechten, Questor. Revs. Lee and TenEyck were appointed a committee to draft and report rules of order and of business. The time of the Semi-Annual Meetings was fixed for the last Tuesdays of April and October of each year. This order at the Spring Session in 1839 was changed to the " Third Tuesdays of the same months." The Classis then adjourned to meet in regular session at the Church of Montgomery, on the last Tuesday (29th) in October next."

THE FIRST MEETING OF THE CLASSIS

after its organization was in " Extra Session " at Montgomery, September 17th, 1833. Rev. R. P. Lee, presided. A call from the Church of Fallsburgh upon Rev. John Gray was presented and approved. Then, as the record has it : "The Rev. John Gray from the Independent Church of England, having produced Constitutional testimonials—having signified his acceptance of the call, and his readiness to subscribe the Formula, It was *Resolved*, "That the Rev. John Gray be a member of this Classis." It will be noticed that nothing is here said about any examination of Mr. Gray as to his theological attainments and views, but we are left to infer that he was received into the Classis upon his credentials merely ; an oversight which, if committed then, has never been repeated by the Classis. But I am inclined to think that the Record is defective. Mr. Gray came before the Classis, not merely as from " the Independent Church of England," but as a member in good and regular standing of the Classis of Schoharie. Dr. Corwin's " Manual " gives the name of but one Rev. John Gray, who, as he states, came from England in 1833, and began his ministry in this country at Fallsburgh in that year. But in the minutes of the Particular Synod of Albany for 1833, the name of John Gray appears as that of a minister without charge in the Classis of Schoharie. I infer that these two John Grays are identical, and therefore that the Classis of Orange received him not on his credentials as a minister of the English church, but on his certificate of dismissal from the Classis of Schoharie. I have referred to this matter because the point is one on which our Classis has always laid great stress and excercised especial caution, and I am loath to have her well-earned reputation in this respect marred by a mistake at the outset. Classis arranged for the installation of Mr. Gray on the 22d of October, which day proving stormy the services were held on the 23d.

THE FIRST REGULAR MEETING

of the Classis occurred according to adjournment, October

29th, 1833, at Montgomery. The roll of Classis on this occasion was as follows :

CHURCHES.	MINISTERS.	ELDERS.
MONTGOMERY,	R. P. Lee,	P. Mould.
BEREA,	J. B. TenEyck,	C. Dill.
BLOOMINGBURGH,	S. VanVechten.	
NEW HURLEY,	T. H. Vandevere,	J. Ostrander.
SHAWANGUNK,	J. H. Bevier,	J. Jansen.
WAWARSING,	A. J. Swits,	Jno. Brodhead.
NEW PROSPECT,	J. W. Ward,	A. Anthony.
FALLSBURGH,	J. Gray.	J. Seaman.
WURTSBORO',		W. Kuykendall.

Of these clerical founders of the Classis one-half are gone to a higher service.

REV. R. P. LEE, D. D.

was born in Yorktown, Westchester Co., N. Y., in 1803. He graduated at Dickinson College in 1824, and at the Seminary at New Brunswick in 1828, and was licensed by the Classis of New York soon after. During a portion of the succeeding year he did missionary work in New York City, and in 1829 received and accepted a call from the church of Montgomery. Dr. Lee was an eminently successful minister. He was not brilliant or learned, but he had few superiors in solidity of judgment and practical executive skill. He had a fine person, an impressive manner and a strong, well-managed voice. His discourses were never sparkling, but were always clear, pointed and weighty with thought. He had great power in prayer, and his holy living was always a commentary upon his preaching. As a counselor of his brethren he had few equals. His opinion upon disputed matters in Classis was the end of strife. Viewed from an earthly stand point, his death, coming as it did, just as he seemed to have reached the perfection of his powers, was a great calamity to the church.

REV. J. B. TENEYCK

was a native of Kingston, Ulster Co. He was educated in the Academy there and at Union College where he graduated in 1818. In 1821 he graduated from the Seminary at New Brunswick, and was licensed by the New Brunswick Classis immediately after. In 1823 he began labor with the newly formed church of Berea which soon called him to the pastorate. The church was an offshoot from a neighboring Presbyterian body and great efforts were made to secure its adhesion to the Presbytery. But Mr. TenEyck laid his influence in the scale of the Classis and decided the struggle. The church was received into the Classis of Ulster, May 6, 1823. I have not been able to learn the exact date of Mr. TenEyck's ordination and installation. His settlement had the old-fashioned element of perpetuity in it. The "Golden Wedding" of Pastor and People occurred early in 1872. Mr. TenEyck had an exceedingly social nature, a warm heart, refined by grace, a sensitive conscience and a ready sympathy with his fellow men. He excelled as a pastor, winning his way to all hearts and always justifying the confidence reposed in him. His genial, cheerful ways made him a favorite among his brethren, while his unaffected modesty and prompt discharge of all duties commanded their respect. He served the Classis for seventeen years in the office of Stated Clerk. The first Volume of the Minutes of Classis is wholly in his handwriting, and about one-half of the second. Mr. TenEyck died April 20th, 1872, after a short illness.

REV. SAMUEL VAN VECHTEN

was born in Catskill, August 4th, 1796. He fitted for college at Kingston Academy, and graduated at Union College in the year 1818. His theological course was finished at New Brunswick in 1822, and he received his licensure from the New Brunswick Classis the same year. For two years following he was engaged in missionary service in the Mohawk Valley and in Central New York. In 1824 he was installed over the united churches of Bloomingburgh and Rome, now Mamakating. In 1829 this union was dissolved, and Mr. Van-Vechten's labors were confined to the Bloomingburgh church till his dismissal in 1841. Out of the number of those who joined the Bloomingburgh church during his pastorate six at least became ministers of the gospel, and all of them have served, or still are serving, the churches with great efficiency. After leaving Bloomingburgh Mr. VanVechten labored for three years as pastor of the church of Fort Plain. Dismissed from there on account of failing health, in 1844, he retired to Fishkill, where he has since resided. During the troublous times which marked the close of his Bloomingburgh life, I have not learned that his christian character was called in question. He differed from his brethren in opinion; they thought the difference to be such as ought to exclude him from the ministry in the Dutch Church; he thought it was not, and fought for his standing with acknowledged ability, and, as the result proved, with success. The weight of increasing years, and the debility of decaying physical powers have brought with them a mellowness of spirit and a ripeness of graces that make Mr. VanVechten's last days his best days. With the patience of hope he is waiting for his change to come.

REV. F. H. VANDEVERE, D. D.

is a graduate of Union College in the class of 1821. He finished his theological course and was licensed at New Brunswick in 1823. He was pastor at Hyde Park in Dutchess Co., from 1823 to 1829, at New Hurley from 1829 to 1839, at Newburgh from 1839 to 1842, and at Warwick from 1842 to the present time. Dr. Vandevere was evidently the Nestor of the Classis during his connection with it. He has a clear head, a profound acquaintance with theological science, a deep love of truth, and a vigorous will. Those who attended the debates with which the great VanVechten war was carried on, will remember the fiery earnestness, and massive force with which the Dr. pushed on the fight. "And there were giants in those days."

REV. JOHN H. BEVIER

was born in Wawarsing in 1805. He pursued a course of study under the oversight of Rev. Dr. C. D. Westbrook, graduated at the Seminary at New Brunswick in 1831, and received his license from the Classis there. In the same year, he was ordained and installed at Shawangunk, where he remained till 1843. He then took the editorship of the Christian Intelligencer which he retained till 1852. Meantime in 1851 he had been installed pastor of the church of Fordham, where he continued till 1853, when he went to Glenham. His pastorate there lasted till 1860. Thence he removed to Rensselaer where he wrought till 1863. From 1864 to 1867 he was pastor of the church of Rosendale. Then for two or three years he acted as Stated Supply at New Concord. Failing health compelled him a year or two since to relinquish the ministry and he is now living in retirement at Hyde Park, in Dutchess Co. Mr. Bevier is a sound theologian, a good sermonizer, and has a good deal of intellectual strength and acumen. He has a nervous organization, and is somewhat eccentric in his ways. He has lived a useful and honored life.

REV. ABRAHAM J. SWITS

is a graduate of Union Colledge, class of 1817, and of New Brunswick Seminary, class of 1820. He was licensed by the Classis of New Brunswick in 1820, and for a year or two did missionary work in the northern part of the State. He became pastor of the united churches of Schaghticoke and Tyashoke in 1823 and remained there till 1829. In that year he was installed over the church of Wawarsing, and dismissed in June, 1835. From 1837 to 1842 he was pastor of the 2nd Church of Glenville, since which he has been living without change at Schenectady. Mr. Swits is a man of some angularities, but genial and large hearted. His sermons have a practical turn and his sentences are more forcible than polished. He is afraid of no man, and always drives straight at his mark. He retains much of his youthful vigor and freshness of feeling notwithstanding the weight of his three score years and ten. *"Serus in Coelum redeat."*

REV. JOHN W. WARD

came into the church from the Presbyterian connection, and I have been able to learn nothing concerning his earlier days. He was installed at New Prospect in May, 1832, and dismissed April 25, 1837. From 1839 to 1841 he acted as Stated Supply for the church of Wawarsing. From 1841 to 1845 he was pastor at upper Red Hook. From 1849 to 1854 he was settled at Green Point. His death occurred in 1859. Mr. Ward was a man of more than ordinary ability, somewhat sluggish in temperament, but moving with great momentum when roused. Meek, placid, and retiring under ordinary conditions, yet his trumpet gave no uncertain sound in the day of battle.

REV. JOHN GRAY

was born in Aberdeen, Scotland, in 1792. For fifteen years he preached as a missionary in Tartary, and among the destitute in the waste places of England. He came to this country in 1833, and the same year was installed pastor at Woodbourne. The church there was in an enfeebled condition and it did not take long with the good dominie's impetuous Scotch zeal to get matters into a fearful snarl. He was impatient, and the consistory was slow. He was exact and the Consistory could not be punctual. Hence, in a year the two were so far apart that the Classis cut the cord that bound them, to the great relief of both. After a succession of subsequent settlements, Mr. Gray died in 1865. But Mr. Gray was no common man. He was self-educated, a man of indomitable energy and determined will. He was a deep thinker, and had great facility of expression. As a paragraphist for the religions papers he developed rare talent, Christ was his Alpha and Omega, and all his effort was to make him known.

THE MEMBERSHIP OF THE CHURCHES

comprised in the new Classis (except those of Shawangunk, New Prospect and Fallsburgh, which make no returns) as reported in the minutes of Synod for 1833 was 880. Of these Montgomery, the largest, had 447, and Mamakating, the smallest, had 11. The geographical limits of these churches were essentially the same as now. The church of Wawarsing has since been contracted more than any other. At that date her boundaries covered the territory now occupied by the churches of Grahamsville and Kerhonkson in part, and Ellenville entire. The church of Walden has trenched somewhat on the grounds of Berea and Montgomery, and more recently the Wallkill Valley church has nestled down between Walden, New Hurley and Shawangunk.

The present enormous sweep of our boundary lines is the result of subsequent accretions. The churches of Walpack, Minnisink and Deerpark were annexed July 24th, 1835. The Neversink region came in in 1849–50, and the annexation of the German field began in 1852. The extremes of our territory from East to West are to-day 80 miles apart, and from North to South are 70 miles apart. Diagonally across this large district from N. E. to S. W. runs the Shawangunk range of mountains constituting a barrier which renders any equable division of the Classis impracticable, and at the same time greatly hinders our intercourse. The question of separation has several times came up in Classis, but it has never been favorably entertained. Our geographical position seems to forbid it. No dividing line can be drawn which will not leave some of the churches to many inconvieinces. Any practicable partition would mass the stronger churches and leave the feebler ones scattered and overburdened. At present the entire subject of division seems to be put indefinitely at rest by the new Railroad routes which traverse the district.

But at the time of its organization, the Classis was compact in territory, and homogeneous in population. The great majority of her church members were "to the manner born." For the most part they knew her history, they comprehended her claims, and cordially accepted her standards ; they were used to her forms and preferred her polity. Doubtless it was true then as now, that a great deal of their attachment to the church on the part of many was the outgrowth of tradition or habit. Many who adhered to her fellowship neither comprehended her excellencies, nor prized her advantages. Nothing had occurred to call their attention to the value of a connection with a church which gave ample scope and facility to all christian endeavor, and at the same time hedged out all reasonable pretext for uneasiness and complaint. Hence, widespread in the church was an external conformity which lacked enthusiasm and zeal.

But this evil was counterbalanced by a virtue. The membership of our churches generally had not itching ears. They had little curiosity about new creeds and new measures. They had tried the old paths, and were content to walk in them. They preferred quiet and safety to uproar and risk. It was a time of fierce excitements abroad. Other branches of the orthodox church were greatly disturbed. Agitators and would-be reformers were going up and down, ringing great bells, and crying with loud voices. What was old and tried was being broken up and flung into crucibles to be melted over   But the Dutch Church, phlegmatic and staid, had no sympathy with these seditions, and no confidence in the movers of them. She was not inclined to controversy, and never indulged in it except in defence of what she held to be the law of truth and order. Her standards led her in a safe "median line" between Antinomianism on the one hand and Arminianism on the other. As she had turned her back upon the dead formalism of the "True Dutch Church," and spewed its blind fatalism out of her mouth, so she set her face as a flint against the vagaries of a rampant New-School-ism, and rejected with persistent scorn its disorganizing theories. And still this avoidance of extremes on both hands, was not the outgrowth either of indifference or cowardice. Her own creed was positive and definite, and her devotion to it was unquestionable. And she had never been afraid to stand by her convictions. Her old "Coetus and Conferentiae war," and her later struggle with "manifest destiny," in the shape of English preaching, had shown that the true Netherlandish blood in her veins, was not much diluted. Her peaceful temper was not born of cowardice. Hence she presumed on being let alone. Her constitution fenced out of her pulpits those ecclesiastical "Wills-o'-the Wisp," the peripatetic evangelists that held up their rushlights and blew their ram's horns at the East and at the West. Her hospitality was not broad enough to cover that variety of tramps. It was not, therefore, probable that the torrent of outside contention would flow across her borders. And even if it did wash the edges of the church at large, this new Classis, it seemed, would be secure. Her laity were intelligent, honest and loyal. Her ministers were of one mind, sound in the faith, devoted to their work, and were in such close contact that dissentions could not grow between them. Thus, the launching of the new Classis was upon smooth waters, and with a clear sky overhead.

At this first regular meeting of the Classis, little business was done besides completing the organization. The committee appointed for that purpose reported a set of Rules which were discussed and adopted. The Lemmata prescribing the order of business were agreed to, and the mode of electing the Stated Clerk and Questor, by a majority of ballots cast, was fixed upon. Among the rules adopted was this: "Four ministers and four elders of Classis shall constitute a quorum, but a smaller number may adjourn from day to day, and endeavor to secure the attendance of absent members." This unwitting interference with a prerogative of the Constitution attracted the attention of the Particular Synod at its next sitting, and the Classis was ordered to erase it.

The second of the above mentioned Rules provided for the presiding officers of Classis as follows:

" He who officiated as Clerk at the last Stated Meeting of Classis shall preside at the next Stated Meeting ; and the members of Classis shall officiate as Clerk in the same order in which they subscribed the formula ; and if any member fail to fulfill this office in his turn, he shall not officiate again until it falls to him by original order."

This practice was continued till April 20, 1852, when this rule was rescinded and the two officers made elective.

The Stated Clerk and Questor have been elected annually at the Fall Sessions. Rev. J. B. TenEyck served as Stated Clerk from the organization of Classis till October, 1851, a period of eighteen years. He was succeeded by Rev. W. S. Moore, who served till September, 1856, five years. To him succeeded Rev. C. Scott, who served till his dismissal, April, 1866, a period of ten years. The present Stated Clerk, Rev. E. W. Bentley, succeeded Mr. Scott.

Rev. S. VanVechten, was elected Questor of Classis at its first meeting and served till 1841, eight years. Rev. R. P. Lee succeeded Mr. V. and served till 1851, ten years. To him succeeded Rev. M. V. Schoonmaker, who served till 1869, eighteen years. Rev. L. L. Comfort served from 1869 to 1871, two years ; Rev. W. S. Brown from 1871 to 1874, three years. Rev. C. Brett succeeded Mr. Brown.

At this first regular meeting, also Rev. Thomas Edwards who had for three years been acting as Stated Supply of the Mamakating church applied for admission as a member of Classis. The reply to his petition is as follows :

Resolved, That Rev. Mr. Edwards have leave to withdraw his papers. That whilst Classis cannot receive him on constitutional grounds as a member of this body : yet from their personal knowledge of the Rev. Mr. Edwards, who has labored for three years within our bounds, they believe him to be sound in doctrine, and exemplary in his practice, and calculated in some spheres to be useful as a preacher of the gospel." Our wonder at the deftness with which this left-handed compliment is paid, is perfected when we find that six months later Mr Edwards "had been ordained and installed pastor of the church of Coeymans." What had become of the "constitutional grounds" in the meantime does not appear, nor are we informed of the precise difference as "spheres" between Coeymans and Wurtsboro. The incident is noticeable simply as illustrating the great caution used by the Classis in admitting strangers into her fellowship.

And now having seen the Classis thoroughly organized for its work, I pass to the consideration of general topics.

BENEVOLENCE.

Our records show a steady growth in this christian grace among the churches. The Classis has taken persistent pains from the beginning to awaken and foster a spirit of liberality.

At the first regular meeting the following resolution was passed :

Resolved : That the inquiry be made of each minister in reference to the plan pursued in his congregation for raising money for the benevolent institutions of the church."

The scriptural duty and method of giving have been exhibited from time to time, and objects of benevolence have been pointed out. The wants of the spiritually destitute at home and abroad have been laid before the churches, and the duty of contributing to them has been freely urged upon the hearts and consciences of our people. Here at home new churches needing the fostering care of Classis have been organized, and feeble ones sustained and encouraged, while the wants of the heathen in the far ends of the earth have not been overlooked.

Our people are not impulsive ; it might be better if they were more so. And yet giving, as most of them do, upon principle and not from caprice, their bounty can be depended upon from year to year. We keep what we gain, and have therefore only to look forward, forgetting those things which are behind. Measured by the Master's rule, we confess to delinquency, but, as the denominations too generally do, "comparing ourselves among ourselves," we think God for the steadiness with which our churches stand up to their work. An occasional panic in the money market, or the failure of a harvest may diminish for a little the flow of their bounty, but the banks of the channel fill again as soon as the drouth ceases. And this has been their peculiarity from the beginning until now. The action of General Synod on all matters of church extension and the spread of the gospel has received the prompt and hearty endorsement of the Classis. It is indeed possible that when the number of our churches and the sum-total of our membership is considered, the average of our contributions may fall below that of some other Classes whose church rolls are shorter. But numbers are not a fair test of church strength. Our Classis has no metropolitan congregations, and but few—three or four at most—strong churches. On the contrary the majority of them have hard work to procure their own living. Life is to them a struggle, and their contributions to benevolent purposes are true "widow's mites." There is no justice in dividing the pecuniary burdens of the church on the basis of the footings of the statistical tables. Willingness and ability are not always commensurate.

FOREIGN MISSIONARY WORK.

The first Licentiate of Classis was one of her own sons, who gave himself to the missionary work in a foreign field, and who, although compelled to bring his worn-out body home to die, left his heart behind him in the wilderness with the few sheep which he had there gathered into the fold. Another missionary still in active service, was maintained part way through his educational process by the churches of this Classis. And when Synod in its wisdom cut the denomination loose from its alliance with the American Board, Classis cordially sanctioned the step, and entered promptly into the work of sustaining our own Board. The sum-total of our contributions to the cause of Foreign Missions during the ten years ending April, 1874, is $21,083 47.

DOMESTIC MISSIONS.

The Classis' work of Domestic Missions has been somewhat peculiar. No sooner was her organization effected than she began the work of caring for and nursing the feebler churches within her bounds. For a succession of years the ministers of Mamakating and Fallsburgh derived a portion of their support from the contributions of Classis. And at the same time efforts were made to establish new churches wherever openings could be found. In 1835 the churches of Walpack, Minnisink, and Mahackamac, now Deerpark, were received from the Classis of New Brunswick, and thus a wide field of missionary effort was opened up. In 1835 the Newburgh church, and in 1839 the Walden church were added to the enlarging bounds of the Classis. In 1844, Classis by her committees explored the region around the head-waters of the Neversink with a view to relieve in someway the destitution which prevailed in that newly settled district. This action led to the creation of the Grahamsville church in the same year, and that was followed five years later by the birth of the churches of Claryville and Brown's Settlement. This field, then lying on the edge of the second great forest in the State of New York, presented all the difficulties of pioneer life. In one instance the iron castings of a saw mill in this region were about that time carried in, a distance of six miles, on the shoulders of the enterprising owner : while his wife followed pluckily at his heels loaded with her only feather bed.

The church of Claryville was organized in 1849 with sixteen members, and that of Brown's Settlement in 1850, with fifteen members. But they were not strong enough to support a minister either alone or together, and if they had been united with Grahamsville they would have made a field too laborious for any one man to cultivate. Hence the result of our efforts there cannot be regarded as a success. One of those churches is a memory, and the other is very like a ghost.

The German field in the Western part of Sullivan County, early enlisted the interest and efforts of the Classis. The church of Jeffersonville organized in 1852, opened the door for protracted and trying labor in all that region. The records of the Classis for the twenty years between 1852 and 1872 will show that that work consumed more of the time and attention of Classis at its regular sessions than all other subjects combined. The older members of Classis will recall the budget of German troubles laid upon the table of Classis at almost every meeting. Perchance they will also remember the bundles of good advice which we used to send back in return ; the queer questions which we answered, the complaints, childish and otherwise, which we adjusted ; the moneys we voted, and the committees we "resolved" into being, and some of us will recall the long rides in snow and mud, in rain and sunshine, across the bleak Sullivan hills, which we took to organize and reorgaize that which somehow refused to stay organized.

Nevertheless, the Germans in that section have done well. They labored in those days under many and great disadvantages. They were very poor, the small capital which they brought with them was exhausted in the purchase of their lands ; their rough farms just hewn out from the hemlock woods yielded more stumps than corn, more bushes than grass, and more bears than sheep. The "bread and butter" problem was serious and pressing, and the salution of it left little space for attention to spiritual and moral wants. Another difficulty lay in the dissimilarity of their habits of thought and modes of working. They had been trained in widely different schools. The Prussian, the Swiss, the Bavarian and the Hollander could not all at once be fused into intelligent Americans. Their notions of the relations between Church and State were ingrained and yet utterly impracticable in their changed condition. And thus they needed to be led almost as children along the untried paths of our Republican habits, and the intricate ways of our Voluntary System.

Another and a severer obstacle lay in their inability or their unwillingness to take anything upon trust. That which they could see and feel and handle, they could believe in, but everything beyond that was unreal and therefore uncertain. Their aversion to debt in monied affairs, seemed to end in an aversion to faith in spiritual things. As they did not like to ask for credit, so they were loath to give it. So long as the Classis would indorse God's promise to sustain them in building up the church, so long it passed current among them, but where Classis stopped they wanted to stop also. And doubtless in our zeal to help them we went too far. We indorsed too often and let the indorsement lie too long. When at last we withdrew our signature and threw them back upon the bare promise, they began to gather strength. God sent them a worthy pastor, and then sent them wisdom enough to be content with him. And to-day he finds a cheerful support which he dearly earns from a prosperous people. Twenty-five years have wrought a great change in all that region, and the prospect now is, that another quarter of a century will place those churches among the foremost in Classis.

For many years our work of Domestic Missions was carried forward independently of the Domestic Board of the church. This occurred through no disloyalty to the denomination and by reason of no distrust of the Synod's chosen agency. It was merely making a neighbor of him who lived next door to us, or rather providing for our own household. The hand of this destitution was reached out to *us*, and we simply put our alms into it. And thus before we were aware we had upon our hands an informal missionary work of no mean proportions. Without at all intending it we seemed to have entered into a rivalry with the Synod in the work of church extension. How to cease from this apparent competition without at the same time surrendering all direct oversight of a field that had come to have a strong hold upon our sympathy and interest, was a question anxiously asked and seriously considered. The difficulty was finally met and obviated by a proposition from the Synod's Board, which was accepted in Classis, January 24, 1855. Under this arrangement all monies raised in Classis for the Domestic Missionary cause are paid into the treasury of the Domestic Board, and the Classis is allowed to say what portion of these shall be expended within her own bounds. On the other hand the Board is not obligated to lay out upon our field any sums which the Classis does not furnish. During the last five years the Classis has given to Domestic Missions $5,014.50.

As respects the other Boards of the church, the Classis will claim that she has borne her full share of the burden of sustaining them. The Bible and the Tract Cause, and other outside benevolent agencies have also reaped generous harvests within our bounds. The temperance cause has uniformly received the fostering care of Classis. Numerous resolutions endorsing and commending its principles and calling upon the ministers to advocate them, are found upon the records. The observance of the great anniversaries of prayer for the general welfare of Zion, for Colleges, for Missions, for the World's conversion, etc., is repeatedly urged upon the churches. And thus in all particulars has the Classis sought to keep abreast of the church universal in its progress toward a final triumph. She has put upon record an intelligent and positive opinion regarding most of the topics which from time to time have agitated the christian public mind.

LOYALTY

The record of the Classis concerning this christian duty is unstained. She has uniformly recognized "the powers that be" as "ordained of God," and has given to them her due subjection and support. She has been loyal to the State. During the late war of the Rebellion, the Classis shared in the general agitation and anxiety. The conflicting views and feelings of that stormy period gave rise to some confusion, and possibly to some temporary bitterness. But the law of mutual forbearance prevailed, and the churches all came through it undivided and harmonious. None of our ministers were directly unsettled by it, and none of our churches were permanently weakened by it. The Classis on all proper occasions spoke out decisively in favor of the national honor and life.

Again, the Classis has always been loyal to the Denomination. She has never allowed herself to be a clog on the wheels of denominational progress, but has been intelligently interested and active in all measures tending to advance the importance and efficiency of the Dutch Church. At her first regular meeting in 1833, she gave a unanimous vote in favor of the Revised Constitution that year adopted ; and again, in 1873, she adopted unanimously the ·· Amended Constitution." The ·· proposed " article relating to the *Deputatus Synodi*, was stricken out by a vote of eighteen to six, and that relating to the Heidelbergh Catechism. was stricken out by a vote of thirteen to ten.

When the question of changing the name of the Church came up in 1867, the Classis indorsed the action of Synod by a vote of nineteen to nine.

In 1864 the General Synod determined to increase the ·· Permanent Fund " of the church by an addition of $20,000. Our quota of this amount was rated at $966 55, which was promptly raised and paid over to the treasurer of the Synod.

It has always been a matter of principle, no less than of pride with the Classis, not to come short in its pecuniary obligations, but this transaction has involved us in seeming delinquency. Our position in the case is, however, briefly this : Down to 1857, certain expenditures of the Board of Direction, such as deficiencies in the Professors' salaries, outlays upon the buildings at New Brunswick, and the running expenses of the Synod, were all classed under the head of ·· Contingent Expenses," and paid out of the income of the Permanent Fund. But at that time (1857) these expenditures had increased and arrearages accumulated, beyond the capacity of that income to cover them. and the policy was adopted of making annual assessments upon the Classis to cover this deficiency. The magnitude of these assessments increased till the Classes were forced to remonstrate. This went on till, in 1864, it was decided to raise the $20,000 above referred to. It was supposed that the income of the fund thus enlarged would suffice for these deficiencies, and leave only the real "contingent expenses" to be met by annual apportionments. It was contended that the Classes would cheerfully pay the moderate annual outlays of the Synod in doing its routine work, inasmuch as they were pretty uniform in amount, and the nature and necessity of them was well understood. The Classes were distinctly informed that having once paid their quota of this $20,000 they should hear no more about "contingent" expenses, except so far as their proportion of the ten or twelve hundred dollars needful to keep the Synod in running order was concerned. But our quota of the $20,000 was scarcely warm in the treasury when the same old cry was ringing in our ears. Synod had made a mistake. Forty instead of twenty thousand dollars were needed; and besides some of the Classes had refused to raise their proportion of even that. So late as in June, 1868, only $15,716.73 had been received toward the full $20,000. Notwithstanding this neglect of the Classes, the Synod went on increasing its annual expenses, and, in violation of its own rule, calling *all* its arrearages "Contingent Expenses," and assessing them upon the Classes in such a way as to put those who had paid upon the same footing with those who had not. For instance, in 1867 the "contingent expenses" of Synod amounted to $2,400, one-third of which, or $800, was assigned to the Particular Synod of Albany. Of this sum, the Particular Synod set off 14.5 per cent, or $116.00, to the Classis of Orange. In reference to this assessment Classis took the following ground : Synod by its own action has fixed its annual contingent expenses at $1000, more or less. It has also agreed that its other expenses—those that are not contingent—shall be paid out of the income of its Permanent Fund, which fund it has voted to increase by the sum of $20,000. It also agreed further that when the several Classes shall have paid their quota of this $20,000 increase, they shall be exempt from assessments except for the actual contingent expenses of the Synod. The Classis of Orange has paid its quota of that sum, and is therefore now exempt from all assessments except for 14.5 per cent, *not* of one-third of $2400, but of one-third of $1000, which constitutes the real "contingent expenses" of the Synod. Instead therefore of paying $116, we will pay $50.00, which is a trifle more than 14½ per cent. of $1000. Another thing which Classis noted was this : No credit was given to Classis for the annual interest of the $966.57, which it had paid as its quota of the $20,000. That interest was $67.65, which, added to the $50 that Classis was content to pay, amounted to $117.65, or just thirty-five cents short of the actual assessment of the Synod. Of course Synod could not see the matter from the Classis' standpoint, and so credited us with the $50.00 paid, and charged us with the remainder In 1873 we were charged in the Minutes with an arrearage of $151.68. How long the Synod may find it desirable to waste Printers' Ink upon this annual announcement, cannot be foretold. We are annoyed by it, but still believe we are right in our refusal to pay it. We are doing what we consider to be our duty in defence of the churches under our oversight. We are willing and glad to bear our proportion of the expenses contingent upon the Synod's yearly gathering. And if an increase of the Permanent Fund is needed to meet the enlarging demands of our denominational work, we stand ready to shoulder our part of that burden also, whenever it shall be regularly laid upon us.

JUDICIAL CASES.

The Classis of Orange has had but three judicial cases which have reached the higher courts. Of these, however, two at least have attracted wide attention. The first one in order is that of

MR. ABRAHAM CRIST.

Mr. C. appealed to Classis from a decision of the Consistory of the Church of Montgomery, in a case tried in Consistory, April 29, 1834. From the record it appears that Mr. C. being a baptized member of the Church of Montgomery, but not having become a communicant thereof, requested the privilege of presenting his children for baptism. But a rule of Consistory required that applicants for that privilege should submit to an examination, the nature of which was prescribed in a resolution read to Mr. Crist. He replied saying that he was willing to submit to the examination, but that it would be useless in his case, for he made no pretentions to the "faith" and "piety" mentioned in the resolution. Thereupon, Consistory refused his request. From this refusal he appealed to the Classis.

Classis, by a vote of seven ayes to five nays, decided not to sustain the appeal. From this point the record of this case on the books of Classis is singularly defective and confused. A motion was made to re-consider this vote not to sustain the appeal, pending the consideration of which, the commissioners of the Consistory who were on the floor of Classis to contest the appeal, claimed a right to vote on the motion to reconsider. The President decided that they had such a right. An appeal was taken from this decision of the chair, which was not sustained, and the commissioners actually did vote. The yeas and nays were then called on the motion to reconsider, and the vote resulted in nine ayes to six nays. And here the Classical record stops. As it stands, a vote *not* to sustain Mr. Crist's appeal is reconsidered, and that is all. And what thickens the muddle is that this motion to reconsider is carried by the votes of these very commissioners, who came there to secure if they could, the very decision which they voted to reconsider. How the Synods found their way through the labyrinth, is a matter of astonishment. No mention is made of Mr. Crist's appeal from this action. We could easily imagine him so confounded by the reading of the minutes that he did not know whether or not an appeal was necessary, if we did not find under the head of "Particularia," notice of the appointment of Revs. VanVechten and Lee as commissioners, to defend the Classis from Mr. C's appeal to the Particular Synod of Albany.

At a meeting of that Body in Albany, May 21, 1834, the appeal was tried, and the conclusion reached is stated thus :

Whereas : It appeared to the satisfaction of this Synod that the wife of the appellant is a member in full communion of the church, and that the Consistory refused to allow Mr. Crist to be associated with her in presenting their children for baptism, therefore :

Resolved : That the appeal be, and is hereby sustained.

No record appears in the Minutes of the Particular Synod of any notice of the Consistory's intention to carry the case any further. Still an appeal was taken which was tried by General Synod, at its session in New York, in June, 1834. There it was decided that inasmuch as Consistory had acted in conformity with a recommendation to the churches passed by Synod in 1816, the appeal must be sustained. But at the same time the Synod voted to rescind that recommendation and put another in its place. Doubtless Mr. Crist comforted himself with the thought that he was actually right though technically wrong.

THE VAN VECHTEN CASE.

There had been but little change in the original *personale* of Classis, when this famous contest was inaugurated. Mr. Ward had been dismissed from New Prospect, but was still a member of Classis. His place had been filled by Rev. John T. Demarest, D. D., the only clerical member of the Classis engaged in the controversy still remaining among us. Dr. Demarest was born at Teaneck, near Hackensack, Bergen Co., N. J., October 20, 1813. His preparatory course was pursued at Borland & Forest's Collegiate School in Warren Street, New

York City. He entered Rutger's in 1830, and graduated in course. His theological education was finished at New Brunswick in 1837, and he was soon after licensed by the Classis of New York. In November of the same year he was ordained at New Prospect, where he remained till April, 1850, when he was called to Minnisink. After a two years' service there he accepted the Principalship of the Harrisburgh Academy at Harrisburgh, Pa., whence, in 1854, he went to Pascack, in the Classis of Paramus where his pastorate lasted till his broken health disqualified him from further service in 1867. He remained without charge till 1870, when he was recalled to his old charge at New Prospect. A protracted illness of Mrs. Demarest forced him to ask for a dismissal again after a year of severe labor. Two years and a half later, that church which had so thoroughly learned his worth, for the third time besought his services. It is seldom that the bond between pastor and people becomes so strong as to outlast these repeated sunderings. In the strife that was so early precipitated upon the young pastor he took sides with the majority of Classis, and gave to it the benefit of his fine scholarship, his thorough acquaintance with doctrinal truth, and his firm adherence to the "form of sound words."

Rev. J. M. Scribner was pastor of the newly-formed church of Walden. He was a graduate of Union College in 1833, and of New Brunswick Seminary in 1836. His first settlement was over the church of Schoharie in 1836, whence, in 1839, he came to Walden, where he remained till 1842. For the ensuing five years he was engaged in teaching in Auburn and Rochester. Since then he has been living without charge at Middleburgh, Schoharie County. Mr. Scribner sided with Mr. VanVechten.

Rev. C. C. Eltinge was then at Deerpark. He was a native of Ulster county, a graduate of the old "Queen's College" in New York City in 1812, and of New Brunswick Seminary in 1816. He began his ministry in the Minnisink and Mahackemack churches in 1817, and died at Port Jervis in 1843. He was a man of great vigor, both intellectually and physically. He did not delight in controversy, but could strike heavy blows whenever the defence of the truth demanded them.

Rev. J. B. Hyndshaw was pastor of the Walpack Church. His connection with the Dutch Church seems to have begun and terminated with his pastorate at Walpack. In Classis he was prompt and efficient in the discharge of duty, and was held in high respect by his colleagues. He was President of Classis when the charge of schism against Mr. VanVechten was tried, and acquitted himself with dignity and success.

The first appearance of this case upon the books of Classis is in the minutes of a Special Meeting, held in the Church of Ellenville, February 19, 1839. The meeting was called to act upon a request for the dismissal of Rev. J. H. Duryea from his pastoral charge of the church of Wawarsing. That business attended to, the following Preamble and Resolution were adopted :

Whereas : Reports are in circulation that certain ministers have been introduced into the church of Bloomingburgh of questionable orthodoxy, and that at a protracted meeting lately held there, certain means and measures have been employed contrary to the usages of the Reformed Dutch Church ; therefore,

Resolved : That a committee be appointed who shall visit said church and make inquiries of the minister, and consistory of said church, and such other persons as the committee may judge competent sources of information concerning the orthodoxy of the ministers who have officiated during the late protracted meeting, and the measures which were employed, and to report at the next stated meeting of Classis.

The committee appointed to this duty consisted of Revs. F. H. Vandevere, J. B. TenEyck, and the Elder, David H. Smith of Montgomery. The date of their visitation was fixed for the first Monday of March next, " at 10 o'clock a. m., and if the weather be unfavorable, the next day at 10 o'clock, a. m."

Mr. VanVechten gave notice that he should complain of this action of Classis.

And thus the contest was fairly inaugurated. Of the condition of the church of Bloomingburgh at this time, I glean the following facts from the Records: In 1834, the year after the Classis was organized, that church reported one hundred and fifty members, and the following appears concerning it in the report of the committee on the state of religion : " There appears to be more than ordinary attention to the great concerns of the soul. An unusual anxiety seems to prevail to wait upon and to derive benefit from the ordinary means of grace. Meetings for preaching and prayer are well attended and apparently with deep interest ; the prayer meetings especially are frequently crowded, and often solemn and melting. Individuals have been deeply impressed on the subject of their soul's salvation, and some have in the judgment of charity been borne again."

In 1836, one hundred and fifty-five members are reported, and in 1839, an addition of sixty-two members is given, making at that date a membership of two hundred and forty-eight.

The committee thus appointed, made their report at the regular Spring Session, at New Prospect, April 30, 1839. They had gone to Bloomingburgh on the 5th of March, 1839, and found the Pastor sick and unable to meet them. They had however examined certain members of consistory from whom they learned that during the late protracted meeting the Pastor had been assisted by Revs. Laird, Fairchild, Wood, and Eggleston. Some of these ministers were members of the New School party in the Presbyterian church—a fact, of which some members of Consistory were aware, and others were not. The theological points upon which inquiries were made by the committee, were the " Imputation of Adam's

Sin," the "Atonement," and "Man's Inability." Upon these subjects one Elder affirmed that the preaching of some of these ministers was unsound ; others had not noticed that. All but one of the Elders had known of special attention to the subject of religion before the protracted meeting, and that one knew knothing about it.

It was also affirmed that anxious seats had been used, to which all were in a general way invited, and then some had been specially urged by the ministers going to them personally. Persons had also been encouraged to ask publicly the prayers of ministers and others, for themselves and their friends. The meetings had been continued for two weeks and one day, with morning and evening services, and one week with evening services only.

One of the Elders had understood one of the ministers to say that "the doctrines which one-half of the ministers preached were sending souls to hell by thousands every day."

The committee then go on to say that two of the ministers thus preaching were members of the Presbytery of Hudson, which Presbytery had published a pamphlet, condemning in language, which they (the committee) quote, doctrines contained in the standards of the Dutch Church ; notably, the doctrine of man's inability, in a state of nature, to obey God's law. Of Rev. Mr. Laird, the committee had evidence to show that he was a suspended member of the Reformed Dutch Church of Hyde Park—suspended for affirming that the doctrines of the Heidelbergh Catechism were dangerous—a fact known to Mr. VanVechten when he employed Mr. Laird.

The committee further state that " Anxious Seats " and " Rising for Prayers " are practices contrary to the customs and usages of the Dutch Church, and they deprecate their use as tending to distract men's minds from the *truth* which is God's great instrument of convertion, and. to result in false hopes and the filling of the churches with members which are not necessarilly an element of strength. They close by offering the following resolutions :

Resolved : That this Classis decidedly disapproves of the conduct of the minister of the church of Bloomingburgh in receiving into his pulpit Mr. Laird, a suspended member of the church of Hyde Park.

Passed by fourteen ayes to three nays.

Resolved : That the Classis disapproves of the following measures pursued at the late protracted meeting in Bloomingburgh, viz : The use of anxious seats ; personally urging individuals to use those seats, and encouraging individuals to rise in their places in the church, and request prayers for their friends present or absent.

Resolved : That the introduction of minis'ers into the pulpits of the Reformed Dutch Church who differ in their views and practices from our standards and usages, is decidedly wrong, and cannot be justified by our articles of correspondence with the Presbyterian Church adopted in 1842, inasmuch as the articles referred to contain exceptions with respect to men of questionable orthodoxy.

The report with its resolutions was then adopted.

In addition to this report there were laid on the table of Classis the following papers :

1. A statement from the Consistory of the church of Bloomingburgh, which was however withdrawn by the consent of Classis.

2. A statement signed by twenty-one individuals, styling themselves " members and ordinary hearers of the church of Bloomingburgh."

3. A like statement signed by seven " members and ordinary hearers of the church of Bloomingburgh."

4. A similar paper signed by two acting and one ex-Elder of the church of Bloomingburgh.

These papers were referred to a special committee consisting of Revs. Lee and Bevier, and Elder J. Decker, of New Hurley, who were to report upon them at a special meeting to be held at Bloomingburgh, June 18, 1839, for which meeting they were also to report an order of business.

At that meeting the committee reported, describing the papers and saying that their allegations were of a general nature, and that any definite action concerning them was rendered needless by the decisive utterances of Classis at its last session.

The paper signed by the Acting Elders, they pronounced out of order and recommended that it be withdrawn.

Still there was one charge running through all the papers which needed attention, viz ; that " the preaching in the Bloomingburgh church has been for some time past incompatible with the standards of our church." This charge was confirmatory of a suspicion prevalent in Classis, that the Pastor of the Bloomingburgh church had departed from the faith, and Classis could do no less than give him an opportunity to explain his position, and if he could, refute the suspicion. Hence, they advised the passage of the following resolutions :

Resolved : That the statement in the memorials presented to the Classis at its last meeting signed by thirty-one individuals belonging to the church and congregation of Bloomingburgh, viz : "that in their oppinion, the preaching in their church has been for some time past, incompatable with the standard of the Reformed Dutch Church " is enough to awaken suspicion in the minds of the members of this Classis, that the Rev. Samuel VanVechten, Pastor of said church may entertain views in theology that conflict with our standards.

Resolved : That this Classis on the ground of such suspicion, proceed to interrogate the Rev. Samuel VanVechten, on the following points of doctrine : *First.* Original Sin, embracing imputation and human inability. *Second.* The Atonement, particularly in reference to its nature and extent. *Third.* The New Birth.

Resolved : That the examination be conducted by a minister of Classis : that each question with its answer be penned by the Clerk, and that when the examination is completed the Classis proceed to deliberate and determine upon its character.

Accordingly. Rev. P. H. Vandevere was appointed examiner, and the interrogation began. But a single question, however was put, when Mr. VanVechten asked for time to consider the topics which were thus to be reviewed. This request was granted, and the investigation was adjourned to the next Regular Session in October.

Mr. V. also asked for a copy of the questions which were to be proposed, but this request was denied.

A special meeting of Classis was called at Montgomery, July 23, to arrange for the installation of Rev. J. M. Scribner, over the church of Walden, and the occasion was used to give the controversy a forward push. A charge against Mr. Van-Vechten, of having created a "schism" in the church of Bloomingburgh, was presented, signed by four members of that church, and covering the following specifications, viz: *First,* By false doctrine ; *Second,* By using unusual means and measures ; *Third,* By neglecting in conjunction with the Consistory, to act upon a proposal to take steps for the dismissal of Mr. V. made by certain members of the church ; and *Fourth,* By admitting into the pulpit Robert Laird, a suspended member of the Hyde Park church.

There was also presented an appeal of Elder Lucas Harding from a decision against him by the Consistory of the Bloomingburgh church.

These papers were read, and then it was

"*Resolved :* That a special meeting of Classis be held in the church of Bloomingburgh on the first Tuesday of September next, at 10 1-2 A. M., for the purpose of trying the appeal of Lucas Harding, and also to receive the answer of the Rev. Samuel VanVechten to the charge of schism preferred by Cornelius Brink and others."

Accordingly, at the time appointed the appeal of Elder Harding was put upon trial. The papers in the case as it was tried in Consistory on the 14th of June, were submitted to Classis. From these it appears that Mr. Harding was accused of falsehood in various statements which he had made concerning the difficulty in the church. Evidence to this effect was given to Consistory, when Mr. Harding confessed his guilt, and consented that his confession should be read from the pulpit. Whereupon the Consistory adjourned the trial till after the meeting of Classis on the approaching 18th of June. This adjournment looks at this distance like a piece of sharp practice on the part of Consistory as though they would hold the rod over the recalcitrant Elder's head and put him upon his good behavior at the meeting of Classis. But if they had any such purpose it was a failure, for at that meeting he presented a statement charging unsoundness upon his pastor, but in such an informal way that Classis gave him permission to withdraw it.

Two days after the meeting of Classis, Consistory met again, took up the case where they had left it and proceeded to depose Mr. Harding from his office and to suspend him from the communion. It was from this sentence that Mr. H. appealed, and it was this appeal which Classis was now to try.

After getting at all the facts in the case, and hearing the parties in full, Classis voted to sustain the appeal, and restore Mr. Harding to his office, thus reversing the decision of the Consistory. Thereupon the Consistory gave notice that they should appeal to the Particular Synod of Albany. Revs. Ten Eyck and Vandevere were appointed commissioners to defend the Classis when the case should come up in Synod.

And I may here say that not having access to the minutes of the Particular Synod of Albany, for the year 1840. I do not know what became of this appeal when it reached that body. No further reference is made to it in the minutes of Classis, and it certainly did not reach General Synod.

This matter disposed of, Mr. VanVechten's answer to the charge of public schism was taken up. It was long and minute. He first denies the competence of one of his accusers. She charges him with preaching heresy, and yet has not been to church in two years, and besides is under censure of Consistory.

The indictment is irregular : it should have been made before Consistory, the constitutional guardians of the pulpit.

One count in the indictment is indefinite, not specifying what is objectionable, nor giving time or place of the offense.

Another count is outlawed, the offence not having been complained of within the prescribed period.

The complaint that he had not heeded the request for a dismissal, lies not against him but Consistory, inasmuch as the request was preferred to Consistory and not to him individually.

And further : he was willing to leave whenever the interests of the church demanded ; but who was to decide that point, the large majority who said stay, or the small minority who said go ?

And lastly, the offense of having admitted Mr. Laird to his pulpit had been already adjudicated by Classis. And not that alone, but he stood ready to prove that Mr. Laird, when he came into the Bloomingburgh pulpit, was a minister in good and regular standing in the Presbyterian church with whom we were on terms of correspondence, and he had no right to go behind Mr. L's credentials and examine his record.

If indeed a schism existed it was contrary to his wish and intention. He had preached conscientiously what he believed to be the truth, and the truth faithfully preached was apt to produce schism.

The vote to sustain this answer was lost by fifteen to four.

The trial then proceeded in due form. Mr. V. was allowed to have all questions recorded which he deemed important.

Mrs. E. VanWyck was recommended to withdraw her name from the charges, and did so.

Various witnesses testified to a dissatisfaction existing in the congregation and church, growing out of the management of the protracted meeting. Some were dissatisfied with the doctrines preached, and some with the means and measures used. Mr. VanVechten cross-questioned freely, and then presented a memorial signed by more than two hundred names, together with a certificate signed by a Rev. Mr. Halliday, expressing confidence in Mr. VanVechten. These papers were ruled out as incompetent testimony, and the decision ruling them out having been appealed from, was sustained by a vote of twelve to three. The treasurer of Consistory testified that the thirty-one who signed the charge against the pastor last year paid $107 of the salary, and he thought there would be no difficulty in raising the salary if they drew off altogether. When the testimony was all in, Classis deliberated, and

Resolved : That in the judgment of this Classis there is a public schism in the Reformed Dutch church and congregation of Bloomingburgh.

This resolution was carried by thirteen ayes to four nays.

Resolved : That inasmuch as it is objected by the accused that some of the specifications contained in the charges introduced to Classis, are not sufficiently definite, therefore Classis will not proceed to the further investigation at present. And

Whereas : The accusers have no request to make,

Resolved : That the Classis considers them as having relinquished the case in its present form.

The examination of Mr. VanVechten ordered at the meeting of June 18, was taken up at the Fall Session, at New Hurley, October 15, 1839.

Mr. V. offered a written statement of his views upon the points in question, but it was declined.

He then formally denied the right of Classis to interrogate him ; but said that if Classis insisted he would answer from the Bible and the standards of the church.

Nineteen questions, covering the doctrines of " Original Sin," " Imputation," " Inability," " Election," and " Atonement" were then put and replied to, chiefly by texts of Scripture and quotations from the catechism.

This ended, Mr. V. again offered his written statement which was again rejected by a vote of twelve to eight. The Classis then

Resolved : That the answers of Rev. S. VanVechten instead of being explanatory of his views of doctrine on the subjects proposed by Classis, are evasions and cannot therefore be considered satisfactory.

Resolved : That Rev. S. VanVechten has by these evasions refused to give the explanation of his sentiments required by Classis on the subjects of " Original Sin," the " Atonement " and the " New Birth ; " that according to the penalty contained in the formula for ministers, required to be signed by the Constitution of the Dutch Church, and signed by Rev. S. VanVechten, he is *ipso facto*, suspended from the office of the ministry.

These resolutions were passed by a vote of fifteen ayes to two nays.

Mr. VanVechten gave notice of an appeal to the Particular Synod of Albany.

This appeal was presented to Classis at an extra session, appointed for the purpose, at Bloomingburgh, November 12, 1839. Revs. Vandevere and Lee were appointed commissioners to conduct the case for Classis in the Particular Synod.

The appeal came up in the Particular Synod of Albany at a special meeting called to consider it, November 19, 1839.

The Synod sustained the appeal by a vote of fourteen to four, but made no formal statement of the reasons on which their decision was based. The commissioners gave notice of an appeal to General Synod.

The commissioners made their official return to Classis at a special session, called at Newburgh, December 31, 1839. At this meeting the formal appeal from this decision of Particular Synod, together with a recitation of the reasons and motives for it, was presented and adopted, and then the further consideration of the matter was postponed to the regular semi-annual meeting.

This meeting was held at Newburgh, April 21, 1840. Here another turn to the wheel within a wheel, which seems to have characterized the case from end to end, was given by a paper sent up from the Consistory of Bloomingburgh, asking Classis what they should do. They had tabled charges against a member of the church, of non-attendance upon the services and ordinances, and she had plead sickness in her family previous to the last six months, and since then she had staid away through a suspicion of the pastor's orthodoxy. Classis advised that the first reason was valid so long as it lasted, and that the last one rested on good grounds. Hence Consistory should let the case rest till the suspicions regarding the pastor's unsoundness were confirmed or dissipated. *Our* verdict is : Served them right, for not issuing the case in the lower court before sending it to a higher.

Revs. Ward and TenEyck were appointed commissioners to prosecute the appeal from Particular Synod on the floor of General Synod.

The appeal came up in Synod at its session in June, 1840, and resulted in the passage of the following :

Resolved : That the appeal of the Classis of Orange from the decision of the Particular Synod of Albany be not sustained ; because in the opinion of the Synod, Rev. S. Van Vechten did not so refuse explanation on the points on which he was suspected, as to subject himself to suspension without trial according to the provision of the formula. This resolution was passed by a vote of thirty-seven ayes to twenty-nine nays.

Resolved : That in view of the circumstances of the case, the Classis of Orange be directed, unless the Rev. Mr. Van Vechten shall, by " further explanation," as contemplated in the formula, give them satisfaction respecting his orthodoxy on those points, respecting which there is sufficient ground of suspicion, (for which a full and fair opportunity shall be given him) to cause charges to be regularly tabled against him, and that they proceed to try the same in a regular and constitutional manner.

This resolution passed by a vote of thirty-nine yeas to thirty nays.

To carry out the direction in the above resolution, a special meeting of Classis was held at New Prospect, commencing August 25th, and continuing till the 27th. Mr. VanVechten presented a bulky document discussing at length the direction, as indicated by the phraseology of Synod's resolution, which his examination should take ; and then coming down to the merits of the case, he spread out his views under the three general heads of " Original Sin," " Atonement," and " Regeneration." His views as thus stated, would seem to be a modified calvinism, and are essentially such as were held by the more conservative wing of the New School Presbyterian Church ; essentially those for the holding of which Lyman Beecher, and Albert Barnes, were two or three years before on trial in the Presbyterian General Assembly. They are views which would undoubtedly be indorsed by the great body of " Old School" ministry in the Congregational Church throughout New Eengland.

The document was read and referred to a special committee, consisting of Revs. C. C. Elting, R. P. Lee, and J. T. Demarest, and the Elders N. Millspaugh, of Walden, and R. Har-

denbergh of Shawangunk. They reported that the prelimi-
nary portion was irrelevant : that his views of Original Sin
and Imputation, while not as strong as could be desired, were
still not discordant with our standards ; that his views of Inability conflicted with those standards, and that his views of
New Birth were indefinate. They therefore recommended the
following :

Resolved: That Mr. VanVechten be now interrogated on
the above-named subjects ("Human Ability," the "Atonement" and "Regeneration.")

To seven questions which followed, Mr. V. successively
answered :   " I take exception to an oral examination." He
then asked that these questions might be put in writing, and
promised to give written answers to them in as short a time
as possible. This request was refused and he asked that the
refusal might be put upon the record. It was then

Resolved : That the above questions be furnished to Mr.
V., and that he be required to give verbal answers to them
this evening at 8 o'clock.

Of the answers returned in compliance with this order, Classis
decided that four were satisfactory, two unsatisfactory, and
two evasive. It was therefore decided that these last four questions should again be put and answers demanded. But Mr. V.
again objected to an oral examination. He was then allowed
to put in any written statement touching the business in hand
which he pleased to offer.

Mr. V. thereupon in writing adverted to the rejected
answers in order, and asked to be informed specifically wherein
they were defective. He did not mean to evade a direct and
full reply, and if Classis would point out the evasion he would
do his best to satisfy their minds. He closed by saying : 'If
the Classis wish me to give my views more at length in writing, I am perfectly willing to do so, if time is allowed me, or
if time be not allowed, that changes be tabled according to the
direction of General Synod."

The whole matter was then referred to a committee consisting of Revs. Lee, Vandevere and Eltinge, and the Elders Manle and Hardenbergh. They, after reiterating the dissatisfaction of Classis with the examination, and quoting the authority of the Formula, recommended the adoption of the following :

Resolved : That Rev. Samuel VanVechten be, and hereby is, declared to be *ipso facto,* suspended from the office of the ministry.

This report and resolution were adopted ; ayes twelve, noes, two.

And so the planet had revolved and again come round to its aphelion. Of course an appeal was the next thing in order. Mr. V. gave the usual notice and Classis adjourned.

On the 4th of September following, within the constitutional ten days, Mr. V. notified the president that he should complain to General Synod of the action of Classis at the foregoing meeting. This complaint was presented to Classis at a special meeting held at Port Jervis, September 22, and was ordered to be entered upon the minutes.

Having thus insured the regularity of his own complaint, Mr. VanVechten immediately put in a written request that he might be allowed to withdraw it, and substitute for it a complaint covering the same ground much more fully, but signed by J. M. Scribner, minister, and G. S. Corwin, elder, constituting, as they styled themselves, "a minority of the Classis of Orange," and directed not to *General* but to *Particular* Synod, an extra meeting of which was called for October 14, 1840, at Albany. Classis consented to the exchange, and the new complaint was read. It was a formidable document containing thirty-one specifications carefully elaborated.

In addition to this Mr. VanVechten give notice of a complaint, signed by himself as pastor, and G. S. Corwin, elder of the church of Bloomingburgh, directed to the Particular Synod, and covering the acts and proceedings of Classis in the case from 1838 to the present time. It is wise for the soldier to be well armed. If the rifle misses, the blunderbuss may not.

Revs. Lee and Vandevere were commissioned to defend the Classis against the appeal, and these two complaints in the approaching session of Particular Synod.

The Synod took up the cases at its meeting on the 14th of October. It refused to entertain the complaint of the " minority of Classis," on the ground of irregularity, in that due constitutional notice of it had not been given to Classis. Mr. V. gave his customary notice of an appeal from that decision to General Synod.

Mr. VanVechten's own appeal from the decision of Classis suspending him from the ministry, was then tried and sustained by a vote of eleven to six. From this decision the commissioners of Classis, in their turn, gave notice of an appeal. Having thus got the case safely into General Synod, Mr. V. withdrew the complaint of the pastor and elder of the church of Bloomingburgh. It was not only a spare gun but a useless one now.

The Classis, at its regular session in the Shawangunk church, October 20, heard the report of the commissioners, drew up and adopted an appeal to the next Stated Synod of General Synod, and appointed Rev. J. T. Demarest and Rev. C. C. Eltinge to prosecute it.

An extra meeting of General Synod was called at Albany, November 10, 1840, " for the purpose of trying an appeal of a minority of the Classis of Orange, from the decision of the Particular Synod of Albany, in October, 1840, and to attend to any business in the case of the Rev. Samuel VanVechten."

" On motion, it was

Resolved : That in view of the peculiar importance and difficulty of the matters expected to come before this Synod, the Synod will spend an hour in devotional services."

The Synod then proceeded to the trial which resulted in the sustaining of the appeal by a vote of fifty to two.

Then came a memorial of which no record was made in Classis, addressed to General Synod, and signed by Rev. S. VanVechten, and concurred in by the Consistory of the church of Bloomingburgh. So much of this as exhibited the theological views of Mr. V. was referred to a special committee, consisting of Revs. James Lillie, Jno. Knox, D. D., Jno. Van Wagenen, and the Elders William B. Crosby and Richard V. Dewitt, who reported the following:

Resolved : That though there are some exceptional expressions in the statements of the Rev. Samuel VanVechten, yet the explanations given by him of his doctrinal views on the subjects of original sin, the atonement and regeneration, are, in the judgment of this Synod, satisfactory, and such as should entitle him to the confidence of the Dutch Church. This report was adopted by forty-six ayes to ten noes.

The following resolutions were then adopted:

Resolved : That the minority of the Classis of Orange be requested to withdraw their complaint now on the table of Synod, and that the Classis of Orange be requested by this Synod to refrain from prosecuting an appeal from the recent decision of the Particular Synod of Albany, restoring Rev. S. VanVechten to the exercise of the ministry, and that thus all further agitation of the case may cease.-

Thus matters stood till at a special meeting of Classis held at Bloomingburgh, January 26, 1841, Mr. VanVechten was dismissed from his pastorate there, upon a joint application of himself and his Consistory.

The regular Spring session of Classis convened at Berea, April 20, 1841. At that meeting the resolution of General Synod, counseling an arrest of proceedings against Mr. V., and also his memorial to Synod explaining his theological views, were referred to a committee consisting of Revs. Vandevere and Eltinge, and the Elder, J. S. Decker, who reported resolutions declaring Mr. VanVechten's explanations to be still unsatisfactory, and that Classis felt itself bound to prosecute the appeal. These resolutions were passed by fourteen ayes to two nays. Revs. Eltinge and Demarest were named commissioners to conduct the case for Classis in General Synod, and Revs. Vandevere and Bevier in Particular Synod, "should their services be needed."

In the Particular Synod of Albany in session at Schenectady, May 5, 1841, it was

Resolved : That, as the sense of this Synod, it is competent for the minority (of the Classis of Orange) to present their complaint immediately to General Synod.

Acting upon this instruction, the minority appeared on the floor of Synod, at Albany in June, 1841, and had their complaint referred to Synod's committee on " Overtures and Judicial Business," who reported that the complaint, although dated nearly a month after the proceedings complained of, was yet in order, because Classis had voluntarily received it as a substitute for one of which seasonable notice had been given. This report was adopted and the trial began.

When the papers in the case had been read and counsel heard, it was decided to arrest proceedings, and take up the appeal of Classis from the decision of Particular Synod, till having brought that up to the same point, the two could be adjudicated together. This done, Synod resolved not to sustain the appeal of Classis for reasons which it states, and to sustain the complaint so far as the same reasons are applicable. It declined to decide again the matter of Mr. Van Vechten's theological views, inasmuch as it had once examined and aproved them. It also gives credit to the purity of intention on the part of Classis in its prosecution of the case.

This conclusion was reached by a vote of forty-three to twenty-one.

These results of Synod's deliberations were, at a special meeting of Classis, held at Newburgh, July 27, 1841, put into the hands of a committee to report upon at the next regular session. Meantime, Mr. V. had received and accepted a call to the Reformed Church of Fort Plain, and at this meeting asked to be dismissed to the Classis of Montgomery. Classis decided to give him his dismissal but not the customary recommendation as being in good and regular standing.

At a special session of General Synod, held in New York in September, 1841, a memorial was presented, signed by the Consistory of the church of Fort Plain, and by Mr. Van-Vechten, narrating the facts of Mr. V's position, and of Classis refusal, and asking relief. This paper went to Revs. Peter Labaugh, R. D. VanKleek and Elder Geo. Zabriskie, as a special committee. By their advice, Synod directed Classis to give Mr. V. a certificate in the usual form, and recommended him to the confidence of the churches.

By the time (October 19, 1841,) Classis was in condition to act upon this direction. Mr. V. had been received by the Classis of Montgomery, and installed over the church of Fort Plain, notice of which fact had been given to the public through the columns of the *Christian Intelligencer.* Classis adverted to this action, and declared that it rendered any further proceedings on its part superfluous.

From this point, this protracted and much-tried case disappeared from the floors, both of Synods and Classis, and the churches had rest. The church of Bloomingburgh remained in a distracted condition for a year or two, when it settled quietly down upon the Rev. Dr. S. W. Mills, then a mere youth, fresh from the seminary, but who was divinely enabled to mingle so much of the wisdom of the serpent with the harmlessness of the dove, that the roiled and restless waters presently became clear and still. It is, however, doubtful if that church has even yet fully recovered from this terrible contest. Though the wounds have healed the scars remain. The bitterness and jealousies of such a warfare are long-lived. In this case a rival organization of another name, taking advan-

tage of this strife, came in and divided the ground, and weakened the forces of the afflicted church ; friends were alienated,
enemies gratified, spirituality deadened, and the growth of the
church hindered for years. Though its health is now fully
restored, it is doubtful if its old vigor is regained. The shock
was too severe.

THE CONNITT CASE.

This case, now one of the "*Canses Celebres*" of ecclesiastical jurisprudence, made its first public appearance at the
regular Fall session of Classis, October 20, 1868, when a communication was received and referred to the committee on
Judicial Business, signed by certain persons calling themselves
"Consistory and members of the church and congregation of
New Prospect." The committee reported, describing the
paper, and adverting to Mr. Connitt's absence, from Classis advised that a committee should visit New Prospect, confer with
the parties and report to Classis at an adjourned meeting to
be holden at New Prospect, on the 17th of November. This
report was adopted, and Revs. TenEyck and Schoonmaker,
and Elders John Lyon and H. Crowell were appointed as
such committee.

At the time and place appointed, the above committee reported that they had visited New Prospect, on October 30,
and conferred with certain members of the Consistory, but
not with Mr. C., who, in a written communication to the committee declined to be present, and gave his reasons therefor.
This communication was included in the committee's report,
the reading of which was interrupted to hear verbal statements of Elder Parliman and Mr. Connitt, who were both in
Classis. When these were heard, the committee resumed the
reading of their report, advising that the parties be urged to
seek a separation. This report was adopted.

The case was next touched in Classis at its regular session
in Newburgh, April 20, 1869. Mr. C. then put in a state-

ment of the fact that his Consistory had declined to discharge the duties of their office. Subsequently, at the same meeting, Mr. C. withdrew this paper, and preferred a charge of faithless desertion of office against certain members of Consistory, who had refused to discharge the duties of their office, so long as Mr. Connit remained Pastor of the church. The Classis ordered this charge to be put in readiness for trial at an adjourned meeting of Classis to be holden at New Prospect, May 3, 1869.

At that meeting a committee consisting of Revs. Mandeville, Comfort and Brown, and the Elders Lyon, Tannery and Millspaugh, was appointed to confer with the parties, and endeavor to settle the dispute. The committee reported that their efforts were in vain. Classis then proceeded to trial. The charges having been read, it was voted to lay them on the table, on the ground of irregularity in the form of them. The following resolutions were then passed :

Resolved : That the Elders and Deacons be recommended to resume their official duties.

Resolved : That the Classis do, in virtue of its inherent power and duty in the case of the churches, hereby dissolve the Pastoral relation between Rev. G. W. Connitt, and the church of New Prospect.

Mr. Connitt gave notice of an appeal to the Particular Synod of Albany, and Rev. G. H. Mandeville was appointed a commissioner to defend Classis in the Synod.

The Particular Synod of Albany met in Schenectady, May 5, only two days later than the action of Classis. Mr. C. sent up his appeal and asked to have its consideration postponed till the next regular session of Synod, in 1870. This request was granted.

The next Sabbath, May 9, Mr. C. entered the pulpit as usual, and read a paper stating that his appeal stopped all proceedings just where they stood previous to the action from which he appealed, and that therefore he was and should be pastor of that church till his appeal was issued.

He, or those acting with him, next barred the church, or caused it to be barred, against the Consistory, who meantime had resumed the discharge of their duties. The Consistory formally tendered him the amount still due on his salary for which they demanded a receipt in full, and also the keys of the church, and the book of Consistorial minutes. He receipted for the money as for so much on salary account, but refused to give up the keys and records. Thereupon Consistory fastened the church, which they meantime had forcibly entered, against him. He, either in person or by proxy, opened it and continued his Sabbath ministrations. His audiences were small, and, as was affirmed, confined chiefly to his personal adherents, and those who came out of curiosity. The Consistory protested against this course, and informed him that on Sabbath, July 4th, they should place in the pulpit a minister of their own selection. On that Sabbath, Rev. Jno. A. Staats, a member of Classis began the regular order of service in the church, but was interrupted by Mr. Connitt who entered the pulpit and read a paper affirming that he was still pastor of the church and proposed to defend his rights as such. He protested against Mr. Staats intrusion, and against any interference with his rights on the part of anybody.

Mr. Staats then appealed to the Consistory present for advice, who informally told him to give way, in order that the scandal of a conflict in the house of God on the Sabbath might be avoided ; whereupon Mr. S., the Consistory, and the greater portion of the audience left the house, and Mr. C. conducted the remainder of the services; at the close of which he gave notice of a meeting of Consistory to be held the following day for the election of a new Consistory. Accordingly, at the time and place appointed, Mr. Connitt and one deacon met and elected persons to fill what they called the " unexpired terms " of two Elders and one Deacon. On three successive Sabbaths Mr. C. announced to the congregation that these would be duly installed in office on the 25th of July, unless they were properly objected to.

These proceedings of Mr. Connitt were officially communicated to Classis by the Consistory at a meeting of Classis held at Walden, July 19. At the organization of that body on that occasion, Mr. C. entered a written objection to the admission to it of Mr. David Parliman as delegate from the Consistory and church of New Prospect. The objection was overruled, and Mr. Parliman admitted by a vote of seventeen to one. Mr. C. also objected, and wished his objection noted; to being called as "without charge."

The special committee consisting of Revs. Van Zandt and Comfort, and the Elder William Crowell, to whom the communication from the Consistory of New Prospect was referred, reported, recapitulating the facts, declaring Mr. C's claim to the pastorate to be illegal, and affirming that even if it were valid, his method of maintaining it was scandalous. They then advised the passage of a resolution, enjoining him to give up the keys and books and to desist from all attempts to exercise the functions of pastor of the church of New Prospect. This report was adopted by a vote of sixteen to three. Mr. C. appealed to Particular Synod.

On the 25th of July Mr. C. proceeded to install the newly elected members of his so-called Consistory into office.

On the 2d of August the clerk of Mr. C's so-called Consistory sent to Rev. J. H. Frazee who had been appointed by Classis to supply the vacant pulpit of New Prospect, on the second Sabbath in August, a communication protesting against his discharge of that duty, and declaring that if he did so, it was at his (Mr. F's) peril.

The next movement in the case occurred August 24, at a meeting of Classis at New Prospect, where Mr. C's complaint of, and appeal from the action of Classis at its late meeting in Walden was read and ordered to be forwarded to Particular Synod.

50

Mr. C. was then ordered to produce the book of minutes of the New Prospect Consistory. To this he replied that the book was not in his possession, and in answer to a further order, declined to say who had them in charge.

At this stage of the proceedings the Sheriff of Ulster County appeared and served upon Revs. S. W. Mills, A. B. Van-Zandt, and M. V. Schoonmaker, copies of a Summons and Complaint, issued by the Supreme Court of the State of New York, forbidding them in any way to interfere with Mr. C. in the discharge of his duties as pastor of the church of New Prospect, and commanding them to show cause why an injunction should not be issued. Mr. Mills at once vacated his seat during the discussion of Mr. Connitt's case.

A communication from the Consistory of New Prospect, narrating the acts of Mr. Connitt done in violation of the order of Classis at its meeting in Walden, was referred to a committee consisting of Revs. Van Zandt, Ten Eyck, and Bentley, who in their report condemned Mr. C's course in general, as a violation of the orders of Classis; and especially his appeal to the civil courts, as an offense against christian courtesy and truth, and advised that a charge of insubordination and contumacy be at once brought against him. This report was adopted by a vote of fourteen to two. The charge recommended, covering nine specifications, was then regularly presented by the foregoing committee.

At the meeting of General Synod. June, 1869, the Classis of Orange was transferred from the Particular Synod of Albany to that of New York, and the Stated Clerk was directed to have Mr. C's appeal also removed in conformity with this change of jurisdiction. He was also directed to put the charge in order preparatory to its trial.

The Classis met in adjourned session at New Prospect (Sept. 7, 1869) to hear Mr. C's answer to the charge preferred. He was again ordered to produce the minutes of the New Prospect Consistory; but he stated in a written reply that he neither possessed nor controlled the book. He was then asked to say who was clerk of Consistory at the time he was dismissed, May 3d? He replied again in writing, that Mr. David Parliman would claim so to be. He was also asked who then (Sept. 7) had the book? He answered, the Clerk of Consistory. These evasions and refusals were declared to be insubordinate and contumacious.

Mr. C's answer to the charge was then read, and Classis adjourned to meet for trial at New Prospect, September 29th, 1869.

At that meeting Mr. C. put in a formal protest against the further prosecution of the case on the part of Classis, which was set aside by vote of Classis. He then in a written statement disavowed any disrespect to Classis in refusing to appear and defend himself. Rev. J. B. TenEyck was then appointed to conduct the case in his behalf. The papers in evidence were read and the witnesses heard, when it was voted that the charge and all its specifications were sustained, and that Mr. C. be suspended from the exercise of the Gospel ministry till he give evidence of repentance. Notice of this sentence was given to Mr. Connitt by the Stated Clerk, to whom Mr. C. gave notice that he should appeal from it to the Particular Synod of New York.

A committee consisting of Revs. Mandeville and VanZandt, and the Elder Jno. Lyon was appointed to report a minute expressive of Classis' view of the interference of the civil with the ecclesiastical courts in this case.

Mr. Connitt's appeal, as also the committee's report on the action of the civil courts, was read in Classis at its regular session at Port Jervis, October 19, 1869. Rev. A. B. VanZandt was appointed to defend the action of Classis in Particular Synod.

That body met at Yonkers, May 3, 1870. The appeal from the vote of Classis to dismiss Mr. C. was first tried, and was not sustained by a vote of fifteen to five. Then followed in order the trial of the appeal from the injunction of Classis, (July 19, 1869) and that from the vote of suspension, (September 30, 1869) in both of which cases the action of Classis was sustained. Mr. C. immediately gave notice of his appeal to the General Synod on each of these decisions.

General Synod met in June, 1870, at Newark, N. J., and tried the first of the above appeals, and by a vote of eighty-one to fifteen, sustained the decision of the Particular Synod. Mr. C. then withdrew the two remaining appeals.

At a meeting of Classis, held at New Prospect, August 10, 1870, notice was given to that body that in two suits instituted in the Supreme Court by Mr. C. against his so-called Consistory for salary which he alleged was due to him for services rendered between May 3d, 1869, and July 7th, 1870, amounting in principal and interest to $1,199.84; he had obtained judgment; the defendants not having appeared to contest the claim.

A call made by the Consistory of the church of New Prospect upon Rev. J. T. Demarest, D. D., was also presented and approved by Classis. A paper was also exhibited to Classis, signed by Mr. C's so-called Consistory, and directed to Dr. Demarest forbidding his further services in the church, and notifying him that the church of New Prospect would be closed until such time as the present troubles should be pacified.

The Classis then unanimously adopted a preamble reciting these continuous acts of insubordination, and a resolution deposing Mr. C. from the ministry, and susepnding him from the communion of the church " until he shall give satisfactory evidence of his repentance."

This action terminated the case so far as the Classis was concerned. In the civil courts it dragged its slow length along till November, 1871, when two Justices of the Supreme Court gave an opinion against Mr. C., and one in his favor. It was then taken up to the Court of Appeals where, January 18, 1874, the decision of the Supreme Court was sustained.

Mr. C. retained uninterrupted possession of the parsonage at New Prospect till in February, 1874, when he was dispossessed by a legal process. It is understood that he has since given in his adhesion to what is known as the "Apostolic Christian Church." He is now residing in Portland, Maine.

The case in its process attracted wide attention, and the decision of it by the highest tribunal of the State defined more clearly than they had ever been, some points of the relationship between the civil law and the ecclesiastical rights of the churches. Mr. Connitt and the brethren of the New Prospect Consistory have achieved immortality so far as russet covered law books can confer it. The church, so long distracted and rent, has rallied nobly from her trial, and now promises not to be permanently injured by the severe and protracted ordeal through which it was thus called to pass.

The following is a full list of the ministerial changes which have occurred in the several churches belonging to the Classis, together with the dates of their respective organizations :

BEREA.

This church, previously organized as a branch of the Goodwill Presbyterian church, came into the Classis of Ulster, May 6, 1823. The book of minutes contains no record of the ordination and installation of Mr. TenEyck.

Rev. James B. TenEyck was settled not far from the organization of the church. He was in office over half a century, and died April 20, 1872.

His successor, Rev. L. L. Comfort, began his labors here July 1, 1872, and was installed pastor September 17th. Rev. W. H. Gleason preached the sermon from Luke, 16 : 21.

BLOOMINGBURGH.

This church was organized the last Sabbath of January, 1820. Down to 1820 it was united with Wurtsboro in its pastorates.

The first pastor was Rev. Geo. DuBois, who ministered from 1820 to 1824, both here and at Wurtsboro.

Rev. Samuel VanVechten was the next pastor. He was installed in 1824, and was dismissed January 26, 1841.

Rev. S. W. Mills, D. D., was ordained and installed pastor May 30, 1843. Sermon by Rev. John T. Demarest, from Acts, 26:17 and 18. He was dismissed January 19, 1858.

Rev. Jer. Searle, Jr., was ordained and installed September 21, 1858. Sermon by Rev. J. Searle, Sr., from second Cor., 4:1. Mr. S. was dismissed December 2, 1862.

Rev. Hasbrouck DuBois succeeded Mr. Searle. He was installed September 8, 1863, and dismissed May 9, 1866. Rev. A. B. Van Zandt preached at his installation.

Rev. J. H. Frazee was installed November 13, 1866, and dismissed December 28, 1869. Rev. G. H. Mandeville preached the installation sermon.

Rev. R. H. Beattie was installed June 14, 1870. Sermon by Rev. S. W. Mills. Dr. Beattie was dismissed March 12, 1872.

Rev. A. F. Todd was installed November 20, 1872. Sermon by Rev. S. W. Mills.

BROWN'S SETTLEMENT.

This church was short-lived. It was organized by a committee of Classis, of which Rev. D. McL. Quackenbush was chairman, August 5, 1850. It was made part of the pastoral charge of Rev. James E. Bernart who was ordained December 9, 1851, and installed pastor of the church of Upper Neversink, November 21, 1854. It lingered on till, after a sort of post-mortem examination by Classis at its Fall session, October 16 and 17, 1855, it was pronounced dead. It seems sad that it should be so, when we recall the fact that since then the great De Bruce tannery has grown up on its territory, and that with proper nourishment it might be representing us and our Master there to-day.

BUCK BROOK.

This church was organized on the same day (December 8, 1859,) and by the same committee which organized Milesville. It was composed of three elders and three deacons, and nineteen members. It shared the fluctuating fortunes of that exceedingly discouraging field. It lingered on till 1863, when it was declared extinct. Some of its members subsequently found their way into the present Reformed church of North Branch.

CALLICOON, OR THUMANSVILLE.

This church was organized January 31, 1856. The committee of Classis on that occasion was made up of Revs. J. B. Ten Eyck and E. W. Bentley, and the Elder A. B. Preston. Rev. J. B. Ten Eyck preached the sermon. The services were held in a school house. A full Consistory was elected and installed. This church has been more prosperous than any which the Classis has established on that field. There has always seemed to be a sort of sturdy good sense and quiet energy about that people which has enabled them to surmount all their hindrances ; united with Jeffersonville, they shared the services of Messrs. Hone, Riedel, and Boehrer.

After Mr. Boehrer left the field in 1865, they were without regular service for nearly two years.

Rev. H. F. Schnellendreussler was installed their pastor May 7, 1867, by Rev. G. H. Mandeville. Besides his pastorate at Thumansville, Mr. S. held a kind of roving commission to the Germans in all that region. But his stay was brief ; he was dismissed October 20, 1868.

A year later Rev. William Elterich found his way to Callicoon, and the church authorities cautiously permitted him to "exercise his gifts." With a loyalty to Classis, exceedingly gratifying under the circumstances, they applied for permission to keep him at work. A year later Mr. Elterich was put upon probation under the care of Classis, and June 11, 1872, he was installed pastor of the church by a committee consisting of Revs. Spaulding, Bogardus, and Brown.

CLARRYVILLE.

This church, under the name of Upper Neversink, was organized September 12, 1849, by a committee of which Rev. J. G. Duryee was chairman. Eighteen members were in the original organization.

Rev. James E. Bernart served it as Stated Supply from 1851 to 1854. November 21, 1854, he was installed as its pastor. Sermon by Rev. J. Searle, Sr. Mr. Bernart was dismissed April 15, 1856.

Its next pastor was Rev. D. A. Jones, who was installed November 21, 1858. Sermon by Rev. E. W. Bentley. Mr. Jones was dismissed December 24, 1863.

Rev. J. W. Hammond was his successor, June 29, 1864. He was dismissed October 16, 1867.

He was followed by Rev. W. E. Turner, installed February 2, 1868, and dismissed April 16, 1872.

CUDDEBACKVILLE.

A petition for the organization of this church signed by forty-three persons was acted upon by Classis in a special session held at Bloomingburgh, January 31, 1854. This petition was granted, and a committee consisting of Revs. H. Slauson, S. Searle, and C. D. Eltinge, and the Elders P. Swartwout and J. N. Taylor, was appointed to effect the organization. The committee discharged this duty March 13, 1854.

The first pastor was Rev. II. Morris, who was installed September 18, 1855. Rev. R. P. Lee preached the sermon

Rev. H. Slauson addressed the pastor, and Rev. S. Searle the church and congregation.   Mr. Morris was dismissed October 1, 1862.

Rev. Egbert Winter was ordained and installed by Classis, August 11, 1863. Sermon by Rev. Jno. Van Vleck, from Ez., 3 : 17. Mr. W. was dismissed January 9, 1866.

Rev. J. L. Zabriskie was ordained and installed pastor May 9, 1856. Sermon by Rev. S. W. Mills, from second Cor., 5 : 20. Mr. Z. was dismissed June 28, 1870.

Rev. W. E. Bogardus was installed November 15, 1870. Sermon by Rev. G. S. Garretson. Mr. B. was dismissed April 22, 1874.

Rev. John DuBois was installed June 21, 1874.   Sermon by Rev. S. J. Rogers, from Gen., 12 : 8

DEER PARK.

This church was organized in 1737, by Rev. G. W. Maucius, then pastor at Kingston.

The first settled pastor was Rev. J. C. Freyenmost, who discharged the duties of that ocffie here from 1741 to 1756.

The second pastor was Rev T. Romeyn, who served from 1760 to 1772.

Rev. Elias Van Benschoten was the third pastor, from 1785 to 1800.

Rev. John Demarest was the fourth pastor, his term of office extending from 1803 to 1808.

The fifth pastorate was that of Rev. C. C. Eltinge, who was installed in 1816, and died in office in 1843.

Rev. Geo. P. Van Wyck was the sixth pastor. He was ordained and installed February 28, 1844. Sermon by Rev. R. P. Lee, from second Tim., 4 : 16. Mr. Van Wyck was dismissed May 19, 1852.

The seventh pastor was Rev. Hiram Slauson who was installed February 22, 1853, and dismissed October 20, 1857. Rev. M. N. McLaren preached at his installation.

The eighth pastor was Rev. S. W Mills, who was installed February 22, 1857. Sermon by Rev. M. N. McLaren. Mr Mills was dismissed October 17, 1871.

The ninth pastor is the present one, Rev. S. J. Rogers, who was installed April 2, 1872. Sermon by Rev. S. W. Mills.

ELLENVILLE.

The church of Ellenville was organized September 15, 1840.

The first pastor, Rev. S. B. Ayers, was installed September 16, 1841. Sermon by Rev. R. P. Lee, D. D. Mr. Ayers was dismissed April 18, 1854.

The second and present pastor, Rev. E. W. Bentley, was ordained and installed October 4, 1854. The sermon on the occasion was preached by Rev. C. Bentley, of Green's Farms, Ct. Rev. R. P. Lee, D. D., gave the charge to the pastor, and Rev. M. V. Schoonmaker addressed the congregation.

SECOND ELLENVILLE.

This church was organized November 13, 1855. Rev. William Wolff had previously done some work among the Germans in the village and vicinity. But the determining force was the judicious labor of Rev. J. P. Pfister, who came on to the ground in April, 1855, and gathered and arranged the materials.

Rev. J. P. Pfister was installed May 20, 1856, by a committee consisting of Revs. R. P. Lee and H. Morris. Sermon by Dr. Lee. Mr. Pfister was dismissed May 16, 1862.

The church was declared extinct April 22, 1863.

FALLSBURGH.

The original organization of this church under the name of the Reformed Dutch Church of Neversink, took place on the fourth Sabbath of November, 1803. No record of its life remains, though occasional reference to it is made in the earlier minutes of the old Classis of Ulster.

It was reorganized under its present title December 9, 1827, by Rev. William R. Bogardus of New Paltz. Five persons then constituted its entire membership.

Rev. Joshua Boyd supplied as a missionary in 1827 and 1828. For four or five years longer a succession of domestic missionaries were on the ground.

Rev. John Gray was installed pastor October 22, 1833, and dismissed October 28, 1834.

Rev. Ambrose Eggleston was installed in June, 1836. Sermon by Rev. J. H. Bevier, from Jer., 5 : 19. Mr. E. was dismissed April 1, 1838.

The next pastor was Rev. Isaac G. Duryee, who was ordained and installed by Classis, July 13, 1842. Sermon by Rev. S. B. Ayers, from second Tim., 4 : 12. Mr. Duryee was dismissed May 13, 1851.

Rev. C. D. Eltinge succeeded Mr. Duryee. He was installed October 7, 1851, and dismissed February 1, 1853.

Rev. Jeremiah Searle was the next pastor. He was installed December 8, 1853. Sermon by Rev. J. R. Lente. Mr. Searle died in office May 28, 1861.

Rev. G. W. Connitt was the next pastor. He was installed May 7, 1862. Sermon by Rev. E. W. Bentley ; Col., 1 : 28. Mr. C. was dismissed October 17, 1865.

Rev. W. S. Brown was installed May 17, 1868. Sermon by Rev. E. W. Bentley.

GRAHAMSVILLE.

This church was organized June 12, 1844, by a committee of Classis, consisting of Revs. R. P. Lee and J. P. TenEyck.

Rev. Thomas Gregory ministered here as Stated Supply, from 1844 to 1848.

Rev. J. W. Hammond was ordained and installed "the third Tuesday of October," 1849. Sermon by Rev. J. B. Alliger. Mr. H. was dismissed May 19, 1852.

Rev. Calvin Case succeeded Mr. Hammond. He was ordained and installed September 8, 1852, and dismissed April 18, 1854. Rev. J. R. Lente preached his installation sermon.

Rev. W. R. S. Betts was installed June 26, 1855. Sermon by Rev. Stephen Searle. Mr. B. was dismissed September 24, 1856.

Rev. D. A. Jones was installed November 21, 1858. Sermon by Rev. N. D. Williamson. On the same day Mr. Jones was also installed over the church of Clarryville, the two being united in one pastoral charge. Mr. Jones was dismissed December 24, 1863.

Rev. J. W. Hammond was recalled and a second time installed over these churches, June 29, 1864. Sermon by Rev. G. W. Connitt. Mr. H. was dismissed October 16, 1867.

Rev. Wm. E. Turner was installed over the united churches February 2, 1868. Sermon by Rev. E. W. Bentley, from Matt., 5 : 13. Mr. Turner was dismissed April 16, 1872.

JEFFERSONVILLE.

This church was organized November 16, 1852, by a committee of Classis consisting of Revs. J. B. Ten Eyck, S. W. Mills, and Elder J. DeWitt.

Their first minister was Rev. William Wolff, who supplied them both before and after their organization. He was never a settled pastor with them, and left them in 1853.

Rev. Julius Hones went on to the field in 1854, and remained till 1858.

He was succeeded by Rev. F. W. A. Riedel, who ministered till 1861.

Rev. John Boehrer was stationed there in 1862. He was

installed over the two churches of Jeffersonville and Thumans-ville, May 28, 1862, and dismissed August 1, 1865.

The church was extinguished by vote of Classis, April 16, 1867.

In 1871, (June 11,) a reorganization was effected by a committee of Classis consisting of Revs. C. Spaulding and E. W. Bentley, and Elder Matthew Jansen.

Rev. William Elterich was installed over the church June 11, 1872, by a committee consisting of Revs. C. Spaulding, W. E. Bogardus, and W. S. Brown. Sermon by W. E. Bogardus, from Acts, 20 : 28.

KERHONKSON.

This church was organized as Middleport, and its name changed October, 1870. It was set in order by a committee of which Rev. S. B. Ayers was chairman, March 9, 1853. The original number of members was eleven. Rev. Ephraim Depuy served it as a Stated Supply in 1856. Its first settled pastor was Rev. N. W. Jones, who was installed November 12, 1857. Sermon by Rev. L. L. Comfort. Mr. Jones was dismissed October 16, 1860.

Rev. John VanVleck was installed September 9, 1862, and dismissed April 20, 1864.

Rev. John Du Bois was installed September 16, 1866. Sermon by Rev. E. W. Bentley ; Col., 1 : 28. Mr. Du Bois was dismissed June 2, 1874.

MAMAKATING.

This church was organized May 7, 1806, under the auspices of the old Classis of Ulster. Lawrence Tears, Willhelmus Knykendall and Peter Crans were members of its first Consistory.

Its first regular pastor was Rev. George DuBois, who served from 1820 to 1824.

From 1824 to 1829 they were supplied statedly by Rev. S. Van Vechten, who divided his services during this period between Wurtsboro and Bloomingburgh.

From 1831 to 1834, Rev. Thomas Edwards was Stated Supply. He never became a member of the Classis.

The fourth minister was Rev. F. T. Drake, who was ordained and installed July 12, 1842. Sermon by Rev. Wm. Demarest, from second Tim., 4 : 1 and 2. Mr. Drake was dismissed October 15, 1844.

He was succeeded by Rev. A. C. Hillman, who was installed July 7, 1846, and dismissed December 4, 1849.

From 1849 to 1853 the church was supplied statedly by Rev. Wm. Cruikshank.

Rev. Stephen Searle was ordained and installed pastor November 22, 1853. The sermon on the occasion was preached by Rev. H. Slauson, from Rom.. 11:13. Mr. Searle was dismissed December 30, 1858.

Rev. John DuBois succeeded Mr. Searle. He was installed August 9, 1859, and dismissed November 9, 1865.

Rev. J. H. Frazee was Stated Supply from 1866 to 1870.

Rev. E. G. Ackerman was ordained and installed May 10, 1870. Sermon by Rev. E. W. Bentley, from second Kings, 13 : 14. Mr. A. was dismissed October 20, 1874.

MILESVILLE.

This church was organized December 8, 1859, by a committee of Classis, consisting of Revs. Jer. Searle, Sr., E. W. Bentley and C. Scott. The church began with three elders and three deacons and thirty-one members. It was ministered to with more or less of regularity by Revs. Hones, Riedel and Boehrer during the periods of their service in that vicinity. The church, never extinct, was resuscitated under the care of Rev. Wm. Elterich, and upon his settlement as their first regular pastor, (June 12, 1872) it assumed the title of the Reformed Church of Fremont, under which it now appears in the minutes of General Synod.

MINNISINK.

Here is another of Dominie Mancius' handiworks. He seems to have traveled down the old "King's Highway" some time in the summer of 1737, and made up a batch of churches like so many loaves, and having leavened and raised them, set them in the oven trusting to somebody else to see that they did not dry or burn up.

Of course Dominie Freyenmost did not keep his hands off. When the Minnisink loaf needed turning he was there to turn it. His bishopric was as indefinite as the Indians birth place, "from Cape Cod to Nantucket and all along the shore." If any of Dominie Mancius' loaves did chance to get a little crusty and dry it must not be charged to Dominie Freyenmost's neglect, but to the physical impossibility of his being in more than four places at once.

Dominie Freyenmost had the oversight of the Minnisink church from 1741 to 1756.

Thomas Romeyn followed him from 1760 to 1772.

Then came the remarkable Elias Van Benschoten, from 1785 to 1800.

Thus far the fortunes of the Minnisink church had followed those of Walpack. But now Minnisink and Mahackamack (Deer Park) joined hands.

Their first minister after this arrangement was consummated, was Rev. John Demarest, who remained from 1803 to 1808.

Then came Rev. C. C. Eltinge, who served the two churches from 1816 to October 31, 1837.

From Mr. Eltinge's dismission onward, Minnisink has been walking alone. Her first pastor under this new order of things was Rev. S. B. Ayers. He was ordained by the Classis and installed June 28, 1838. Sermon by Rev. J. H. Duryea. Mr. A. was dismissed April 20, 1841.

His successor was Rev. Jacob Bookstaver a native of Montgomery, who was licensed by the Classis July 28, 1840, and ordained and installed at Minnisink, January 12, 1822. Sermon by Rev. R. Pitts, from second Tim., 4 : 16. Mr. B was dismissed October, 1847.

Rev. J. G. Morse, a Presbyterian clergyman, served as Stated Supply from 1848 to 1849.

Rev. J. T. Demarest, D. D., was their next settled pastor. He was installed May 14, 1850, and dismissed August 17, 1852.

The next pastor, Rev. David A. Jones was installed May 17, 1853, and dismissed September 21, 1858.

F Rev. Cornelius Gates was installed May 16, 1860, and dismissed April 15, 1862.

Rev. William Cornell was ordained and installed September 2, 1862, and dismissed April 22, 1863.

Rev. William S. Moore was installed June 29, 1864. Sermon by Rev. A. McWilliams. Mr. Moore was dismissed July 19, 1869.

Rev. William E. Turner was installed May 21, 1872. Sermon by Rev. E. W. Bentley, from Rev., 3 : 21.

MONTGOMERY.

The Montgomery congregation is largely of German descent, and their church was originally connected with the German Reformed body. The precise date of its organization seems to be lost. Its earliest records go back to the year 1732, when William Mancius is mentioned as a "Special Supply of the congregation of Wallkill, and regular pastor of the congregation of Kingston." Another entry in another hand shows that the church of Montgomery was organized in 1732,* by Rev. George Wilhelmus Mancius, (the same as above mentioned) of Catsbaan, who served this church as Stated Supply till 1762. There seems to have been sixteen members at the date of the organization, besides the two (one elder and one deacon) who formed the first Consistory. The same names occurred then which are now prominent in the congregation, as "Kraus," now spelled Crans; "Maul," now Mould; "Sinsebaugh," "Christ," now Crist; "Nieukirk," now Newkirk; "Jungblot," now Youngblood; Johannes Jungblot was the first Elder, and Jacob Buchstahder was the first Deacon.

From 1751 to 1768, Rev. John Moffet, pastor of the neighboring "Goodwill" Presbyterian church frequently preached and baptized in the congregation.

In 1751, the church united with the churches of New Paltz and Shawangunk in a call upon Rev. Barent Vrooman, who preached his first sermon under the call September 9, 1753. A year later he left the field.

In 1764 the name of Frederick Mutzelius occurs as an occasional supply. This is doubtless the person of the same name mentioned in Corwin's Manual.

From 1764 to 1771 the church was supplied at intervals by Rev. Mr. Cough of East Camp. Concerning Dominie Cough's life and labors our church records are strangely silent.

From 1772 to 1777, Rev. John Michael Kern officiated as pastor, though no mention is made of his installation.

From 1778 to 1784, Rev. Rynier Van Nest acted either as Stated Supply or as pastor, probably the latter, under a call made in connection with the Shawangunk church.

In 1788, Rev. Moses Freleigh became the pastor and served the two churches of Montgomery and Shawangunk till 1811,

*Dr. Dewitt says 1731.

when he confined his labors wholly to Montgomery, till his death in 1817.

Rev. Jesse Fonda succeeded Dominie Freleigh. He was installed September 28, 1817, and died in the pastorate May 2, 1827.

Rev. R. P. Lee, D. D., was installed July 15, 1829, and died September 30, 1858.

Rev. A. B. Van Zandt, D. D., was installed May 15, 1860. Sermon by Rev. J. B. Ten Eyck. Dr. Van Zandt was dismissed August 28, 1872, to enter upon the Professorship of Theology in the Seminary at New Brunswick.

The present pastor, Rev. Cornelius Brett was installed August 12, 1873. Sermon by Rev. Dr. Van Zandt, from first Cor., 1 : 21—24.

NEWBURGH.

This church was organized on the " third Tuesday of February," 1835. Sermon by Rev. J. H. Bevier, of Shawangunk.

Rev. Wm. Cruikshank, first pastor, was installed, October 22, 1835. Sermon by Rev. J. H. Bevier. Mr. C. was dismissed January 10, 1838.

Rev. J. M. Fisher was installed August 26, 1838, and dismissed January 15, 1839, and asked to be dismissed still earlier. The sermon at his installation was preached by Rev. J B. Hyndshaw.

Rev. F. H. Vandevere was installed July 21, 1839. Sermon by Rev. J. B. Hyndshaw. Dr. V. was dismissed August 23, 1842.

Rev. A. B. Van Zandt was installed December 14, 1842, and dismissed June 5, 1849.

Rev. M. N. McLaren was installed on the evening of the second Tuesday of November, 1850, and dismissed February 24, 1859. Rev. J. B. Alliger preached the installation sermon, from second Cor., 2 : 4.

Rev. G. H. Mandeville was installed September 13, 1859. Sermon by Rev. C. Scott. Dr. M. was dismissed October 19, 1869.

Rev. W. H. Gleason was installed July 19, 1870.

NEW HURLEY.

The first settled pastor of New Hurley was Rev. Stephen Goetschius. The church, organized October 18, 1770, had occasioned supplies and frequent pastoral service from the church of Kingston till Dominie Goetschius' installation early in 1776. It was united with that of New Paltz in the support of the pastor who divided his labors between them. Mr. G. was dismissed August 29, 1776.

Rev. John H. Myer was installed October 13, 1799, and dismissed January 10, 1803. He ministered to both churches and made but a brief stay in that hospitable Dutch neighborhood. Those staid church-going farmers have not a habit of letting a dominie slip through their fingers so easily.

Rev. Peter D. Freleigh was settled in the pastorate of the united churches December 26, 1807, and thus continued until January 16, 1816, when he was called to assume the entire pastoral charge at New Hurley. In November of the same year he was dismissed.

February 18, 1817, Rev. William R. Bogardus became the pastor of the two churches. November 10, 1828, the churches separated, and Mr. Bogardus gave himself wholly to New Paltz.

April 1, 1829, Rev. F. H. Vandevere was installed over New Hurley alone. He was dismissed May 10, 1839.

Rev. William Demarest was installed early in 1840. No mention appears on the minutes of Classis respecting that service. Mr. D. signed the Formula, and his name appears as pastor in the roll of a meeting of Classis held July 28.

But who installed him and when, is not stated in the minutes either of Classis or Consistory. Mr. Demarest was dismissed April 16, 1845.

Rev. Elbert Slingerland was installed on Tuesday, February 24, 1846. Sermon by Rev. A. B. Van Zandt. Mr. Slingerland was dismissed April 25, 1854.

Rev. L. L. Comfort was installed November 2, 1854. Sermon by Rev. J. B. Ten Eyck. Mr. Comfort was dismissed on account of impaired health, April 18, 1871.

Rev. R. H. Beattie, D. D., was installed April 2, 1872. Sermon by Rev. M. V. Schoonmaker.

NEW PROSPECT.

This church was organized October 2, 1815. Its first Consistory was composed of Hazael Van Keuren and Cornelius Brink, elders, and Geo. Niver and James Stott, deacons.

The first pastor was Rev. A. D. Wilson. He was called and settled by the two churches of New Prospect and Shawangunk. He was installed in April, 1816, and dismissed in April, 1829.

Rev. R. C. Shimeal was settled in September, 1829, and dismissed in 1831.

Rev. J. W. Ward was settled in May, 1832, and dismissed April 25, 1837.

Rev. J. T. Demarest was ordained and installed November 23, 1837. Rev. J. H. Bevier preached the sermon. Mr. D. was dismissed in April, 1850.

Rev. W. S. Moore was installed October 2, 1850, and dismissed October 21, 1856.

Rev. William Hamilton was installed May 6, 1857. Rev. C. Scott preached the sermon, from Phil., 2 : 29. Mr. H. was dismissed March 10, 1864.

Rev. G. W. Connitt was installed May 10, 1867. Sermon

by Rev. M. V. Schoonmaker, from first Cor., 1 : 23. Mr. Connitt was dismissed May 3, 1869.

Rev. J. T. Demarest, D. D., was installed a second time pastor September 2, 1870. Sermon by Rev. A. B. Van Zandt, from first Cor., 1 : 21 and 24. Dr. Demarest was dismissed on account of the feeble health of Mrs. Demarest, April 18, 1871.

From 1871 to 1873 the church enjoyed the stated ministrations of Rev. Jno. A. Staats.

September 14, 1873, Dr. Demarest was for the third time installed pastor of this church. Sermon by Rev. F. H. Vandevere.

NORTH BRANCH.

This church was organized June 10, 1871, by a committee consisting of Revs. E. W. Bentley, C. Spaulding and the Elder Matthew Jansen. It had a full Consistory and twenty-eight members.

Rev. Wm. Elterich was installed as its first and only pastor June 11, 1872.

SHAWANGUNK.

The earlier records of this church are lost. Dr. Corwin is however doubtless in error in dating its organization in 1732, designating Rev. Johannes Schuneman as its first pastor. Dr. Dewitt in his discourse at the opening of the North Reformed D. church gives 1751 as the date of organization. Prof. Scott's opinion is that it was organized in 1750 by Rev. Johannes H. Goetschius who was then pastor of the churches of Schraalenburgh, and Hackensack in N. J. It is on record that Mr. G. visited New Paltz in June, 1749, and baptized a child. Again, April 22d, 1750, he was in New Paltz and baptized five children, two or three of whom were from what is now the Shawangunk congregation; and the probabilities are that on his way home from New Paltz he stopped at Shawangunk and ordained a Consistory. The congregation at that time was attached to the pastoral charge of Dominie Mancius at Kingston. As Dominie M. was not then a member of the " Coetus," this invasion of his ecclesiastical territory doubtless met with his protest.* No members of the church of Kingston belonging to this congregation were dismissed to join this new organization till two years later. Still this may have been from the fact that there was no pastor at Shawangunk till 1753. There is no list of elders and deacons belonging to the Consistory till 1860. The record of baptisms begins with April 24, 1750, when four children were baptized, and on the 25th four more by Mr. Goetschius. From this time on the baptismal register is regularly kept, though the ordinance was administered by various hands, till the settlement of a regular pastor. On February 4, 1751, the churches of New Paltz, Shawangunk, and Wallkill, (now Montgomery) united in a call upon Rev. Barent Vrooman. Mr. V. accepted this call, and as the necessity then was, went immediately to Holland for licensure and ordination. The Classis of Ultrecht licensed him June 17, 1752, and ordained him March 6, 1753. There is no record of his installation ; but he preached his first sermon as a pastor August 26, 1753, at New Paltz; at Shawangunk September 2d ; and at Wallkill September 9th. He retained this connection till October, 1754, when having accepted a call to Schenectady, he removed thither.

Rev. Johannes Mauritius Goetschius was the second pastor. He was called to the united churches of New Paltz and Shawangunk January 18, 1760, and began preaching at Shawangunk August 17th, and at New Paltz August 24th of that year. He resided at Shawangunk, died March 17, 1771, and was buried under the North side of the present church edifice there.

The third pastor was Rev. Rynier Van Nest, who was called April 26, 1774. No record of his installation appears, but he began preaching at Shawangunk, November 6, 1774, and at

---

*Corwin's Manual affirms that Dominie Mancius once preferred charges against Mr. Goetschius, to the Coetus. *Query:* Was it on account of *this* invasion of Mancius' bishopric.

New Paltz the next Sabbath, November 13th. For some reason his connection with New Paltz was terminated, and he began preaching at Montgomery, September 27, 1778. March 7, 1785, he was dismissed to Jamaica, L. I.

The fourth pastor, Rev. Moses Freleigh, was called to the united churches of Shawangunk and Montgomery, February 20, 1788. He was ordained and installed in the Shawangunk church May 17th of that year. The sermon on the occasion was preached by Rev. Isaac Blauvelt, of Fishkill. In May, 1811, he was dismissed from Shawangunk, and thereafter confined his labors to the Montgomery church.

The fifth pastor was Rev. Henry Polhemus, who was called by the Shawangunk church alone. His call was dated January 23, 1813; and he was installed June 13, 1813. The sermon was preached by his predecessor, Rev. Mr. Freleigh. Mr. Polhemus died November 2, 1815, and is burried under the North side of the church.

The sixth pastor was Rev. A. D. Wilson. The church of New Prospect, then just organized, united with the Shawangunk church in his call, which was approved by the Classis of Ulster, January 16, 1816. He began preaching under the call February 25th; was ordained and installed April 14th. Sermon by Rev. Peter D. Freleigh. He was dismissed on account of his health April 14, 1829.

The seventh pastor was Rev. Henry Mandeville. The records of Consistory give no account of his settlement further than that it took place in 1829, and that the connection was terminated in 1831. His pastorate was short, but very successful.

The eighth pastor was Rev. J. H. Bevier who was settled in 1831, and dismissed October 18, 1843.

The ninth pastor was Rev. James B. Alliger, whose call was approved at the same meeting of Classis at which Mr. Bevier was dismissed. At a special meeting of Classis held November 21, 1843, arrangements were made for Mr. Alliger's installation " on the second Wednesday of December, proximo, at eleven A. M. Rev. William Demarest was appointed to preach on the occasion. As Mr. A. appears on the minutes of the next regular meeting as pastor, I presume the arrangements were carried out, though no record of that fact is made. Mr. Alliger was dismissed to the South Classis of L. I., December 17, 1850, becoming thus the second pastor which the church of Shawangunk has furnished directly to the church of Jamaica.

The tenth pastor was Rev. Charles Scott. His call was approved at a meeting of Classis held August 5, 1845, and his ordination and installation were arranged for " the second Tuesday of September next." The pertinacity with which the records of Classis adhere to the day of the week and ignore the day of the month, is vexatious in the extreme. " The second Tuesday of September next " came on the 9th, when Classis met. The sermon was preached by Rev. R. P. Lee, from second Cor., 5 : 20. Mr. Scott's long and successful pastorate terminated May 7, 1866, when he was dismissed to accept a professorship in Hope College, Michigan.

The eleventh pastor is the Rev. Cyril Spaulding. He was installed May 28, 1868. Rev. G. H. Mandeville preached the sermon, from second Cor., 2 : 15 and 16.

WALDEN.

This church was organized by the Classis of Orange September 13, 1838.

The first pastor was Rev. J. M. Scribner, who was installed July 23, 1839. Sermon by Rev. J. H. Bevier. Mr. Scribner was dismissed April 20, 1841.

Rev. C. Whitehead, the second pastor, was installed May 10, 1842, and dismissed April 17, 1849. The sermon at his installation was preached by Rev. J. T. Demarest, from Ez., 37 : 1—14.

Rev. M. V. Schoonmaker, the third and present pastor, was

installed August 21, 1849. Sermon by Rev .William Cruikshank, from Eph., 4 : 8—11.

WALLKILL VALLEY.

This church was organized by a committee of Classis of
which Rev. M. V. Schoonmaker was chairman May 11, 1869.

Rev. A. B. Van Z andt preached a sermon from Hag., 1 : 8.
The original members were twenty-five in number.

The first and sole pastor Rev. B. C. Lippencott was installed
April 13, 1872. Sermon by Rev. A. B. Van Zandt.

WALPACK.

This was another of Dominie Maucius' organizations, ac-
complished somewhere about 1737.

The first minister was the ubiquitous Johannes Casperus
Freyenmost, who began his labors June 1, 1741. If he remained here till 1756, as is stated by Dr. Mills in his " Historical Discourse " at Bushkill, he still managed to do a great
deal of work at book-keeping among the records of the Wawarsing church.

Rev. Thomas Romeyn was settled in 1760, and remained
till 1772.

Succeeding him came the eccentric but godly Elias Van-
Benschotin, a name quite as unmistakably Dutch, and vastly
more familiar in the church. thanthe veritable Knickerbocker
itself. He was installed August 28, 1785. He made good
proof of his ministry here till 1800.

Rev. James G. Force was installed November 17, 1811, and
was dismissed in 1827.

His successor, Rev. Isaac S. Demund, was installed December 2, 1827, and dismissed June 13, 1829.

Mr. Demund was followed by Rev. David Cushing, who
served as Stated Supply from October, 1831, to July, 1832.

Rev. Garret C. Schenk was ordained and installed April 6,

1834. Sermon by Rev. S. A. Van Vranken, D. D., from first Cor., 1: 21. Mr. S. was dismissed in March, 1835.

Rev. J. B. Hyndshaw was installed January 17, 1836. Sermon by Rev. J. B. Ten Eyck. Mr. H. was dismissed October 9, 1839.

—Rev. Robert Pitts, licensed by the Classis July 28, 1840, was ordained, and began his labors here as Stated Supply, April 21, 1841, and continued them till 1860, when his impaired health compelled him to resign.

In 1855 the field was divided, and since then two ministers have for the greater part of the time had their hands full in its cultivation, under this new arrangement.

Rev. A. McWilliams was the first pastor of Lower Walpack. He was installed June 1, 1861. Sermon by Rev. William Hamilton. Mr. M. was dismissed May 17, 1870.

The present pastor of Lower Walpack, Rev. J. F. Shaw, was installed December 8, 1870. Sermon by Rev. R. H. Beattie, D. D.

Rev. N. W. Jones was Stated Supply for Upper Walpack for a year beginning in the fall of 1861, and ending in the fall of 1862.

The first and only settled pastor of Upper Walpack alone, is Rev. G. S. Garretson, who was installed May 19, 1863. Sermon by Rev. G. H. Mandeville, D. D., from 1 Cor., 3: 9.

WAWARSING.

This church was organized in 1745, by Rev. Johannes Casparus Freyenmost, then pastor at Port Jervis. The print of his finger is upon everything that was done here between 1745 and 1751.

About that time the church was united with the Rochester church in the settlement and support of ministers.

In 1753 the two churches called Rev. Jacobus Frelinghuysen.

He went to Holland for ordination and died on the return voyage.

In 1755, the Rev. H. Frelinghuysen, a brother of Jacobus, was called to the vacancy. He accepted, preached on his license, waiting for ordination, till 1758, when he was ordained, and two weeks later was dead of small pox.

Rev. Dirck Romeyn was pastor of the United Churches from 1766 to 1775.

From 1782 to 1786 Rev. J. R. Hardenburgh served this extended bishopric.

To him succeeded Rev. Abr. Van Horne from 1789 to 1795.

Rev. Garret Mandeville was the next pastor from 1798 to 1802. He seemed to have confined his ministry to the churches of Wawarsing, Rochester and the Clove, Marbletown being provided for in some other way.

Rev. R. Westervelt succeeded Mr. Mandeville and occupied the field from 1802 to 1808.

After a vacancy of six years Rev. James Murphy, D. D., was installed in 1814, and was dismissed in 1825.

Rev. M. S. Hutton, D. D., was sent to the Wawarsing church by the Missionary Society of the R. P. D. C. in 1827, and remained some eighteen months.

Rev. A. Hoffman served in the same capacity from 1828 to 1829.

In 1829, Rev. A. J. Switz was installed, and remained till June 1, 1835.

Rev. J. H. Duryea was ordained and installed October 30, 1837. Sermon by Rev. F. H. Vandevere. Dr. Duryea was dismissed February 10, 1839.

Rev. J. W. Ward served the church as Stated Supply from 1839 to 1841.

Rev. James Demarest, Sr., was installed April 20, 1842. Sermon by Rev. F. H. Vandevere.

Rev. J. McL. Quackenbush was installed the "third Tuesday of July," 1849. The installation sermon was preached by Rev. R. P. Lee, D. D., from Matt., 28 : 18 and 20. Mr. Q. was dismissed August 5, 1851.

Rev. J. R. Lente was installed December 30, 1852. Sermon by Rev. William Cruikshank, from first Cor., 1 : 23. Mr. Lente was dismissed October 3, 1854.

Rev. N. D Williamson was installed January 29, 1856. Sermon by Rev. J. Searle, Sr. Mr. W. was dismissed May 28, 1861.

Rev. John Van Vleck was installed September 2, 1863. Sermon by Rev. G. W. Connitt. During Mr. Van Vleck's pastorate, the churches of Wawarsing and Middleport were united. Mr. Van Vleck was dismissed April 20, 1864, and died March 14, 1865.

Rev. Miner Swick was installed October 5, 1864. Sermon by Rev. Jno. W. Hammond. Mr. S. was dismissed March 30, 1869.

Rev. J. R. Talmage was installed July 6, 1869. Sermon preached by Rev. G. H. Mandeville. Dr. Talmage was dismissed April 22, 1874.

Rev. Goodloe B. Bell was installed October 12, 1874. Sermon by Rev. E. W. Bentley, from second Kings, 13 : 14.

Licentiates of the Classis of Orange.

The following is a list of ministers who have received their license from the classis :

1. William Youngblood, July 24, 1835.

It is not unmeet that the Classis should have signalized its attachment to the cause of Missions by applying the first exercise of its minister-making power to the person of one who gave his life to the work of preaching Christ to the heathen. Mr. Y. was a native of Montgomery, became a member of the Reformed Church there, graduated at Rutger's College in the Class of 1832, and at the Seminary in 1835, was licensed as above, ordained by the Classis April 26, 1836, and on the 8th of June following sailed for Batavia in the Island of Java. For thirteen years he labored with an enthusiastic earnestness to bring men to Christ. With broken health he returned to America in 1849. He never regained strength enough to undertake any regular service, and after ten years waiting for the Master's call, obeyed it and went up higher in 1859.

2. John Hudson Duryea. Dr. Duryea was a native of Bloomingburgh. He was educated at New Brunswick where he graduated from College in 1834, and from the Seminary in 1837. He was licensed by Classis July 26, 1837.

He was Ordained and installed at Wawarsing, Oct. 30, 1837, dismissed February 10, 1839, and since that date has been pastor of the 1st Church of Totowa, at Paterson, N. J.

3. John B. Crawford was a native of Hopewell, Orange County, N. Y. Educated at New Brunswick, where he graduated at the College in 1836, and the Seminary in 1839. He was licensed by Classis July 23, 1839, was settled at Middletown Village, N. J., in November, 1839, and died a year later. He was a man of great promise and died greatly lamented.

4. Robert Pitts is a native of Bloomingburgh, graduated at New Brunswick in 1837, and was licensed July 28, 1840, ordained April 21, 1841, and as a Stated Supply ministered to the Walpack Church till 1860, since which date he has lived at Stroudsburgh, Pa., without charge.

5. Jacob Bookstaver was born at Montgomery, graduated at New Brunswick in 1837 and 1840, was licensed by Classis July 28, 1840, and ordained and installed at Minnesink, January 12, 1842. He was dismissed from there in October, 1847, and became a teacher at Belleville, N. J., where he died December, 1848. He was a pure-minded, gentle-hearted christian and lived and died greatly beloved.

6. Francis T. Drake was educated at New Brunswick, graduating in 1838 and 1841. He was licensed July 27, 1841, ordained and installed at Wurtsboro, July 12, 1842, dismissed October 16, 1844. He was pastor at Canastota, from 1845 to 1853. He has since then left the church.

7. Alexander C. Millspaugh is a native of Montgomery, was graduated at New Brunswick in 1838 and 1841, licensed July 27, 1841, was pastor at Middletown Village from 1841 to 1866, and is now living without charge at Marlboro, N. J..

8. Aaron B. Winfield was born at Montague, N. J., regularly graduated at New Brunswick in 1839 and 1841. He was licensed August 22, 1842, and went into the service of the Presbyterian church, and died at Paramus, N. J., in 1856. He was an able minister of the New Testament.

9. Rev. Geo. P. VanWyck is a native of Bloomingburgh, was educated at New Brunswick, 1840 and 1843, licensed August 1, 1843, ordained and installed pastor at Port Jervis, February 28, 1844, and dismissed May 19, 1852. Mr. Van-Wyck is now Chaplain in the U. S. Army.

10. Cornelius D. Eltinge, son of Rev. C. C. Eltinge, was born at Port Jervis, and graduated at New Brunswick in 1844 and 1848. He was licensed August 1, 1848. He was installed at Fallsburgh, October 7, 1851, and dismissed February 1, 1853. He is now engaged in business in the State of Illinois.

11. Laurence L. Comfort is a native of Montgomery, graduated at Union College in the class of 1848, and at the Seminary at New Brunswick in 1851. He was licensed August 5, 1851, was pastor at Whitehouse, N. J., from 1852 to 1854, was installed at New Hurley, November 2, 1854, dismissed April 18, 1871, was abroad in pursuit of health for a year, and was installed pastor of the Berea church, September 17, 1872.

12. Rev. John Van Vleck was a native of Shawangunk, graduated at New Brunswick in course, 1852 and 1855. He was licensed August 21, 1865, and served from 1855 to 1859 with distinguished success as Principal of Holland Academy. From 1859 to 1862 he was Principal of the Academy in Kingston, N. Y. September 2, 1862, he was installed pastor at Napanoch, and September 9th, at Kerhonkson. He retained the pastorate of the two churches till April 20, 1864, when his broken health rendered the necessary labor more than he could discharge. During the ensuing year he gradually declined till at midnight, March 14, 1865, he fell asleep. Mr. VanVleck was a ripe scholar, a deep thinker, an excellent sermonizer, a faithful pastor, and a devout christian. Viewed from our human stand-point, the church millitant suffered a sore loss in his transferral.

13. Josiah Jansen was a native of Wawarsing. He was

graduated at New Brunswick in 1856 and 1859, licensed May 26, 1859. For a year he remained unsettled preaching as health and opportunity allowed. In 1861, he was ordained and installed pastor of New Concord, Columbia County, N. Y., and in 1864, resigned and went to his father's house to die. He lingered a few weeks and then expired. He died as he had lived a man, full of faith and of the Holy Ghost. He was well equipped whether for living or dying.

14. Rufus M. Stanbrough is a native of Newburgh. He finished his educational course at New Brunswick in 1858 and 1861, was licensed May 28, 1861, ordained and installed over the Churches of Manheim and Indian Castle soon after, and remains there still.

15. J. Kelley Rhinehard is a native of Shawangunk, was graduated at New Brunswick in 1859 and 1861, and licensed May 27, 1862, and the same year was ordained and installed pastor at Roxbury, Delaware County, N. Y., where he remained till 1873, when he was settled over the Church of Prince-town in the Classis of Schoharie.

16. Louis H. Bahler was a native af Holland, graduated at New Brunswick in 1864 and 1867, was licensed June 25, 1867, and ordained and installed over the Church of Coeymans in the same year.

www.ingramcontent.com/pod-product-compliance
Lightning Source LLC
Chambersburg PA
CBHW021521270326
41930CB00008B/1036